MENTAL HEALTH PROBLEMS
OF WORKERS
AND THEIR FAMILIES

**Volume XI in the Series
Problems of Industrial Psychiatric Medicine**

Series Editor: Pasquale A. Carone, M.D.

MENTAL HEALTH PROBLEMS
OF WORKERS
AND THEIR FAMILIES

Pasquale A. Carone, M.D.

South Oaks Hospital
Amityville, New York

Stanley F. Yolles, M.D.

State University of New York at Stony Brook
Stony Brook, New York

Leonard W. Krinsky, Ph.D.

South Oaks Hospital
Amityville, New York

Sherman N. Kieffer, M.D.

State University of New York at Stony Brook
Stony Brook, New York

Library of Congress Cataloging in Publication Data
Main entry under title:

Mental health problems of workers and their families.

(Problems of industrial psychiatric medicine, ISSN 0277-4178 ; v. 11)
   Based on a conference held Apr. 7–8, 1983, sponsored by the South Oaks Foundation in conjunction with the Dept. of Psychiatry and Behavioral Science, Health Sciences Center, State University of New York at Stony Brook.
   Includes index.
   1. Industrial psychiatry—Congresses.   2. Mental health—Congresses.   3. Family psychotherapy—Congresses.   I. Carone, Pasquale A.   II. South Oaks Foundation.   III. State University of New York at Stony Book. Dept. of Psychiatry and Behavioral Science.   IV. Series.
[DNLM: 1. Environmental Exposure—congresses.   2. Mental Health Services—congresses.   3. Occupational Diseases—psychology—congresses.   4. Occupational Health Services—congresses. W1 PR574M v.11 / WA 495 M552 1983]
RC967.5.M47   1985   362.2   84-10836
ISBN 0-89885-227-7

CONTENTS

5

CONTRIBUTORS

VIRGINIA ACCETTA, R.N., M.S.
Clinical Specialist
Outpatient Department
University Hospital at Stony Brook

MARIE ARPRANO, R.N., M.S.
Clinical Specialist
Consultation and Liaison Service
University Hospital at Stony Brook

FRED B. CHARATAN, M.D.
Clinical Director
South Oaks Hospital

WALTER J. DONHEISER, PH.D.
Associate Director of Psychological Services
South Oaks Hospital

JOHN J. DOWLING, M.D., M.P.H.
Commissioner
Nassau County Department of Health

VINCENT J. GALLAGHER, M.D.
Associate Medical Director
Grumman Aerospace Corporation

NORMAN GOODMAN, PH.D.
Professor and Chairman
Department of Sociology
State University of New York at Stony Brook

IRVING LEE HAMMERSCHLAG, M.D.
Medical Director
Long Island Lighting Company

JEANNE T. HEALEY, R.N., M.A.
Nursing Director, Retired
Corporate Medical Department
Western Electric Company

PATRICIA K. HERMAN, R.N., M.S.
Assistant Administrator
Psychiatric Services
University Hospital at Stony Brook

HOWARD HESS, M.D.
Corporate Psychiatrist
Western Electric Company (AT&T)
Agency Psychiatrist
Port Authority of New York and New Jersey

JACQUELINE ROSE HOTT, R.N., PH.D., F.A.A.N.
Executive Director
Mid Atlantic Regional Nursing Association

HENRY J. KRAETER, M.P.S.
Director of Personnel
South Oaks Hospital

HAGOP S. MASHIKIAN, M.D.
Senior Psychiatrist
South Oaks Hospital

KENNETH B. MILLER, M.D.
Occupational Health Physician
Oil, Chemical and Atomic Workers International Union

ANNE NELSON
Co-Director
Institute on Women and Work
New York State School of Labor Relations
Cornell University

ARTHUR B. SHOSTAK, PH.D.
Professor of Psychology and Sociology
Drexel University
Consultant to Unions and Corporations
on Stress-Relief Programs

DONALD W. SNELLER
Minister
Community United Methodist Church

EDWARD R. SODARO, JR., M.D.
Staff Psychiatrist
South Oaks Hospital

GRAHAM SPANIER, PH.D.
Vice Provost
Professor of Sociology and Psychiatry
State University of New York at Stony Brook

HOWARD A. VAN JONES
Recording Secretary
Director of Special Health Services Committee
Local 504, Transport Workers Union

LEON J. WARSHAW, M.D.
Executive Director
New York Business Group on Health
Clinical Professor
Environmental Medicine
New York University

CHARLES WINICK, PH.D.
Technical Consultant
Central Labor Rehabilitation Council of New York, Inc.

RICHARD M. ZOPPA, M.D.
Senior Psychiatrist
South Oaks Hospital

PREFACE

On April 7th and 8th, 1983, the South Oaks Foundation, in conjunction with the Department of Psychiatry and Behavioral Science, Health Sciences Center, State University of New York at Stony Brook, sponsored a conference, "Mental Health Problems of Workers and Their Families," for mental health professionals and members of labor and management.

In this time of mounting economic and social change, American workers and their families are faced with an array of problems, both in the workplace and at home.

As many at our conference indicated, there is a sense of dread at many worksites and many towns and villages because of the possibility of toxic materials or polluted atmospheres. One study showed that family members of workers at a particular factory were contracting deadly diseases at an unusually high rate. Why? The workers were inadvertently bringing home toxic substances which had permeated their work clothes.

This volume is one in which those with varying viewpoints have an opportunity to come together for a synthesis of opinions. Our speakers and panelists included representatives from many fields of health and the corporate world.

The result of the conference was not to provide easy answers, but to offer a forum for beginning discussions which will, hopefully, lead to solutions. The two-day conference at South Oaks Hospital set the stage for further considerations and further discussions. It was our aim to bring together representatives of various, diverse groups so that a common denominator for working together could be established.

ACKNOWLEDGMENTS

This book is the eleventh in a continuing series dedicated to various aspects of psychiatric industrial medicine. Each year the South Oaks Foundation and the State University of New York at Stony Brook co-sponsor these conferences. Held in the spring of each year, the conferences address themselves to varying topics. Some in the past have included "Alcoholism in Industry," "Misfits in Industry," "Stress and Productivity," and "100 Years of Psychiatry: An Historical Perspective."

This book represents a distillation of the most important parts of keynote speeches and the panel discussions that follow. The book would not be possible without the active cooperation of all the keynote speakers and panelists.

We are indebted to the Board of Directors of South Oaks Hospital who have actively supported these annual conferences since 1971.

We are also deeply indebted to our Executive Assistant, Catherine T. Martens, and our Director of Community Relations, Lynn S. Black.

Chapter 1

AN OVERVIEW OF BOTH THE PERSISTING AND EMERGING PROBLEMS

Arthur B. Shostak, Ph.D.

I sometimes wonder where Will Rogers is now that we need him. I think I may have found where his spirit resides. His spirit resides in a woman we know as Erma Bombeck. In a recent column she was trying to convey the spirit of joblessness. She wrote:

Arthur B. Shostak received his Ph.D. in Industrial Sociology from Princeton University in 1961, and his B.S. in Industrial and Labor Relations from Cornell University in 1958. In 1961, he joined the faculty of the Wharton School at the University of Pennsylvania, and moved in 1967 to Drexel University where he became a Professor of Sociology. He is an adjunct professor with the AFL-CIO's George Meany Center for Labor Studies, and the Education Center of the United Steelworkers Union. Among his 12 books are such titles as *Blue Collar Stress*, *Blue Collar Life*, and *Blue Collar World*. A consultant on the future of work to many unions, he has also consulted on work-related issues with Proctor and Gamble, General Electric, Scott, Univac, and other major corporations. Preoccupied now with advances in computer-based education, Dr. Shostak is attempting to help labor unions learn how to gain mental health aid from this new tool.

The pain isn't anything you can treat or put your finger on. But it's there. Sort of like being kicked by a horse in a phone booth and there's no place to lie down and be sick, and you don't have a dime to call someone. There's a constant sensation of despair like you've just heard you won the lottery but you flushed your ticket down the toilet. You hold an imaginary gun to your head and fire six rounds of guilt every three hours. Your self-worth and self-esteem begin to erode. You feel like a fraud in the eight o'clock traffic—everybody knows you're just dropping off the kids at school, you really have no place to go. People don't respect you anymore. They look at you like a child molester. When you go to lunch and someone else picks up the check, you want to stuff it right up his nose. You hate yourself for becoming hooked on the soaps. You worry about yourself when you clip a horoscope that's optimistic and put it in your billfold even though the paper is three months old. Will people ever stop trying to cheer you up by telling you stories more depressing than yours? Why don't they admit that everybody drank the water in Mexico but you were the only one that got sick? There's a glut on advice...

To be out of work and unproductive is like the last one waiting to be picked for the baseball team. It's a chipped tooth on prom night. It's arriving at the party before the hostess is out of the shower. It's being the only one on the airplane that a fly buzzes around. It's being the child your mother never liked. I give up. It's beyond description.

I want to work with three persisting and, at the same time, emerging matters. I want to argue that we recognize that Will Rogers could have written Erma Bombeck's material in the 1930's and yet the subject has a new dimension now. I have identified it as involving a special type of job loss, job jitters, and job strain.

Well, what's new about joblessness? For one thing, it raises the possibility of something we can call "Depression mentality," an attitude characterized as one where economic loss is converted to a strong sense of personal loss, irrational sense of guilt, and irrational anxiety about the very fact of survival; a new form of Depression mentality. Now, what's new is the backdrop: We have had seven recessions since 1945. Each has left us with a higher level of unemployment than the previous one. We have built up in a step-like fashion to the point today where measured unemployment is approximately 10 percent (and we needn't review the gross understatement of these Federal statistics). Most significant, of course, are situations in Ohio and Illinois where measured unemployment is 22 percent; in Bradfield and Johnstown, and in other communities where the despair is pervasive, insidious, ubiquitous, and without any reasonable likelihood of near-future relief.

And that connects to the word "permanence." What is dramatically new about job loss is the sense on the part of thousands and thousands of men and women across the country that they may not soon gain re-employment, certainly not at the jobs they personally identify with. If you travel as I do—among other things, I am an adjunct educator for the United Steelworkers Union—and hear men and women talk about never making steel again, you may find this strange since some of us think blue-collar workers would welcome freedom from the mill's onerous work conditions. It's not entirely that way. The steelworkers have been nurtured, developed, reared, and raised to identify much of their self-esteem with that mill and that process; the notion that they will never make steel again threatens a rudderless state of personal affairs.

When President Reagan visited Control Data's Pittsburgh operation, where 120 ex-steelworkers were being re-trained, one of the ex-steelworkers broke from the ranks and presented the President with a resumé. He said, "Mr. President, I've been searching for a job for a year. Can you help me?" It was a moment of considerable pathos, one that brought shouts of "right on" from fellow trainees. There is this sense that even the $550,000 Control Data has gotten to operate 20 of these centers nationwide to re-train ex-steelworkers, that all of this is minuscule compared to the scope of the problem, to the numbers of men and woman grievously affected.

So, this nagging sense of loss-of-work permanence can be connected to Toffler's 1972 best-seller, *Future Shock*. We live against the backdrop of that 20-million-copy book, available now in scores of different languages. Even though it was over-written and overdone, it contributed to the language an invaluable tool—the concept of "future shock." Much as Betty Friedan indicates one of her contributions was to "name the disease that had no name," the "feminine mystique," so Toffler gives us the concept of "future shock."

The men and women I'm talking about, the jobless who fear long-term or even permanent joblessness, watch the media sing the praises of Japanese robotics. American companies, in turn, understand you do not make robots to mimic humans; you make robots to maximize machine potential. The arm of the robot does not turn three-fourths, which is all the human elbow and arm can do. The arm of the robot turns 360-degrees because the machine can do that. We continue to dramatically improve our robotics.

Well, the jobless men and women I'm in touch with sense that economically-driven improvements in robotics, in an advanced automation system, are in its ability to re-place 10 typists in three training days with three word pro-cessors. That kind of advancement in the American world of work continues to cement their loss of employment. And they have this sinking sense of permanent, personal obsolescence. Their Depression mentality, in short, has got to be understood with more rigor than we sometimes bring to this "future shock" phenomena.

Most of us, in our research articles, espouse longitudinal data. We really would love to follow up a group that's appropriate, but we seldom do the work; instead, we urge it on our graduate students.

I want to share findings from a seven-year follow-up that two sociologists completed with 250 workers previously employed at a brewery in South Bend, Indiana, a brewery that closed in 1972. By 1979, 233 workers had been relocated. If you were to go to the statistical abstracts to find the death rate for males with the age distribution of the 1972 group, the death rate for that group would have been 9.2 percent. When I spoke recently at a plant closing conference being run by the AFL-CIO, I asked audience members what they thought the death rate had actually been. Their guesses, as you might imagine, were guesses like 12 percent or 18 percent. Actually, the mortality rate was 150 per 1,000; that is, *16 times* the normal mortality rate.

One more statistic. These laid-off ex-brewery workers had been urged to relocate. They loved South Bend, Indiana, however, and by 1979, less than two percent had relocated. Less than two percent. Over the seven years, 52 percent had managed to get back to work, but 77 percent of them were earning less than before the shutdown. (This is the sort of thing that we can only learn from longitudinal work.)

We know, for example, that we have something now called "explosive families." The problem in the 1930's was that men were shocked by the enormity of joblessness— 25 percent of the labor force unemployed; Central Park tent colonies; Times Square one enormous soup kitchen;

the Okies and the Arkies; *The Grapes of Wrath,* and every-thing that went with it. Many became abusive, not only of themselves with substance abuse and suicide, but abusive of people whom they loved, whom they would never in their right minds have treated as badly as they did. Fifty years later, where are we? We have explosive fathers, to be sure, but now we also have explosive mothers. And we have explosive teens. So the syndrome 50 years later—given role confusion, given role stress, given role overload—is the presence of explosive families in our "future shock" America.

The New York Times-CBS News national survey in January 1983 found that 48 percent of families in which an adult has been unemployed in the last year reported a sub-stantial increase in serious acrimonious family quarrels. In 1983, thanks to the work of Louis A. Ferman, a sociologist at the University of Michigan who, for 25 years, has been collecting data on the jobless, we're now interested in what we call "the emotional victim." And we understand in 1983 as we did not in 1933 that the emotional victim is frequently a member of the family *other* than the unemployed person. So now we are interested in what happens to teenage chil-dren as they watch the demoralization of the family's pri-mary breadwinner, male or female.

At Boston College, Dr. Ramsay Liem has completed intense studies of 40 blue-collar and 40 white-collar families in their second and third year of unemployment. This Boston College data suggests wives of unemployed men become significantly more depressed, more anxious, more phobic, and more sensitive about interpersonal relation-ships than do the wives of employed men. While no real surprise, we gain more rigor and specificity from these findings than we've ever had before. Ferman adds that the wives of unemployed men have to meet family needs with fewer resources. They have to stroke their husbands and try to keep the family going. But, Ferman asks in closing, "Who strokes the stroker?"

In 1976, we had 416,000 known cases of child abuse. In 1980, we had more than 700,000 cases, or an increase of 10 percent. The National Committee for the Prevention of Child Abuse argues that the major trigger for child abuse is the social disorganization in families traumatized by joblessness they fear is permanent. In April 1983 we have final figures for only 29 states: child abuse has gone up in 21. Where the unemployment rate is high, as in Oregon with 11.5 percent unemployment, child abuse rates have gone up 25 percent. In a state like Arizona, a Sunbelt state that surprises observers with its unemployment rate as high as 9.9 percent, child abuse rate has gone up 47 percent.

We must add to this overview the fact that, for the first time is recent years, 11 million Americans have lost their health insurance coverage. Joblessness, particularly in the non-union context, results in the loss of medical fringe benefits, our wonderful invention for workers of group fiscal protection against hospitalization costs. In 1982 alone, 11 million people dropped through such a hole in their "safety net." We expect many more families to run out of health insurance coverage if joblessness persists and, as they sense they're running out, they begin to delay medical care—dental care as well as mental health care. So, community mental health centers around the country are reporting an increase in the people coming in for counseling or therapy, but they are coming later than ever with more severe problems than ever before.

And what are you left with? As I move on to my other two topics, you're left trying to determine what you think of the "Job-a-thon." A social invention, it has been used in Cedar Rapids, Iowa; Cincinnati, Ohio; Kansas City, Kansas; Birmingham, Alabama; and Providence, Rhode Island, among other communities. Three hours of prime time television has 200 jobless Americans plead for 10 minutes on the screen for a job. You don't need an afternoon soap opera; you can sit in your living room in the evening, and in 10-minute sequences, one jobless American after another will appear and tell his or her story.

When the station in Providence, Rhode Island, on January 28, 1983, ran a "Job-a-thon" for the first time, the President of the United States phoned to compliment the station for its contribution to the American cultural scene. There were 4,000 applicants for 200 TV spots in the television series, but there are 65,000 unemployed people in the Providence, Rhode Island viewing area. I don't understand how the numbers add up. Of the 200 people who got on the show, 10 were re-employed. The show, however, was so popular that the station has been besieged with letters urging that it be repeated. And the idea is rapidly spreading across the country.

We must worry in our "future shock" America about something called "unemployment careers." Ferman has spent 25 years looking at joblessness, at the onset of emotional illness connected with involuntary unemployment, the doubts, the self-incrimination, the guilt, and the ambivalence about personal worth. All of this can impair future potential in the labor market. Ferman warns that the traumatically displaced worker, on re-employment, can perform at lower productivity levels and with very irregular performance, resulting in dismissal for cause. Ferman says, "Wait, watch, be very attentive." When the newly re-employed go to work, they often earn less than what they previously secured and, thanks to seniority, to downward bumping, and to what is available in the labor market, they seldom return at the status, the prestige level, and at the privilege and perk rank they once knew. At work, we expect them to be grateful, attentive, and fine performers, but, in truth, there are all kinds of reasonable reasons for them to be easily dismayed, ill-humored, overly sensitive, and obvious candidates for dismissal. So, Ferman talks about an "unemployment career"—a downward spiral which can lead to a diminished potential for re-employment.

Let's look now at job jitters. Psychologist Harvey Brenner argues that the losers of work are not even half the problem. A larger problem is posed by the effect of rampant joblessness on people who *continue* to work, people who watch jobs being "exported," "inported," "edported," and "outported."

What do these terms mean? "Exported" is easy. The Atari company recently shocked America by sending 1,500 jobs to Taiwan. Those are 1,500 high-tech jobs. But high-tech was going to rescue us. High-tech was going to sop up structural unemployment in our smokestack, brown field, old line industries. High-tech was going to help create the new America—the information society, in which there would be a place for all of us on an adequate payroll. Taiwan's payroll, however, runs 30 percent less than the West Coast payroll of an Atari plant, and that's very appealing to a company that last year had something like a 30 to 35 percent drop in its share of the market.

Atari isn't alone, of course, in the exporting of low-skilled jobs. High-tech has had a wonderful, glossy reputation, but it may become only a very small number of elitist brain workers, and a much larger number of under-rewarded assembly workers, all employed in non-union paternalistic settings. So, the presently-employed watch jobs being exported.

They also watched jobs being "inported," or lost to advanced automation. We bring in new advanced electronic systems that swallow up their jobs. And they watch jobs being "edported,"or upgraded in educational requirements. In the city of Philadelphia, for example, we expect a college degree from certain people working at the checkout counters in supermarkets. They're told they need this degree because they're looked at as candidates for store manager positions. Perhaps, but there are only so many store managers. And there are a lot of young men and women with bachelor's degrees who would drive cabs if they could not get a checkout counter job. So they'll take those jobs. And when they do, we no longer need the high school dropout or the high school graduate for these positions. "Edported": the artificial inflation of credentials of what were once exclusively blue-collar jobs.

And then there is "outported," or contracting out, a very fast-moving phenomenon. My university, for example, is across the street from a large building of a major electrical manufacturer that took some pleasure in contracting out all of its janitorial services, all of its building guard services, and all of its parking lot services, thereby dismissing a long-standing labor force. The labor force had been unionized, and had managed to negotiate several fringe benefits, considerably above what the contracting service provider offers its workers. And, as the new provider is non-union, when you do not like somebody in the service ranks, you call the contractor, and that somebody isn't there the next day. What we have in contracting out are underclass, not blue-collar or working class adults, but underclass men and women being boosted up into formerly blue-collar jobs. While that may be good for America, it is also hard on the working class. (Particularly if you've got from four to eight million aliens in this country eager for these non-union, no fringe, low-reward jobs. But we don't talk about that especially volatile matter.)

What job jitters has meant, and what is quite relevant to our conference, is the recent predominance of concessionary bargaining. For the past two years, 18 million trade unionists have been *returning* contract term victories—extra holidays, forms of personal latitude at work, forms of fringe benefits—that had once been thought vital and important enough to hard bargain over. The A&P system in Philadelphia, for example, which put 3,500 food store workers on the street over a year ago, has reopened now, and they're all back to work. What the workers agreed to includes three years of wage rollbacks, a reduction of paid holidays, and a contraction of allowable vacation time. Men and women who had worked their way up to two weeks' vacation—that's after 15 years—are back now to only one week. In this very strange climate, the average unionist senses powerlessness on the part of organized labor, once a strategic agency of collective social gain.

We make a lot in this country of what John Kenneth Galbraith calls "countervailing power." It's the American way, the way of checks and balances, and it makes sense to us. But the recession profoundly damages all of this. You get the likes of the United Steelworkers' Union agreeing to a four-year contract with very substantial rollbacks only to discover soon thereafter that the same corporate executives who made such a strong demand for union concessions were also negotiating with British Steel to import steel and lay off even more American workers. My steelworker and steel union friends feel betrayed. The company rushes to explain it's the only way to save the industry. Perhaps. If you want to understand the mental health confusion of the American work force, you must wrestle with the gray, not with the black and white, but with the gray area topic of the steel industry and its concessions/import controversy.

And finally, we have as part of job jitters the fact that the average family income gain in the 1950's was 36 percent for the decade, while in the 1960's, it fell to only 34 percent. But in the 1970's, it fell to 8 percent. Eight percent! We may or may not have inflation under control. You can get economists to argue either side of the question. But what we have had is profound diminution recently of family earning power and of the family well-being of working men and women. And that's a major component of job jitters.

Now, to close this review of what is bothering us, and what is likely to continue to bother us, let me turn to my crystal ball. Job strain, for example, has the following steadily emerging dimensions. The National Institute of Occuptional Safety and Health (NIOSH) and the Occupational Safety and Health Administration (OSHA) from 1970 to date have been my friend and yours. They have helped in many vital ways, including good research and the conversion of initially silly rules into more reasonable regulations. Inadequate staff size, perhaps, but for our purposes, what are NIOSH and OSHA about? They're about consciousness-raising. We used to have Green Cross campaigns, we used to urge attention to the use of steel-tipped shoes and hard hats, and we used to worry about employees who cleaned chimneys—all of this, traditional and useful health and safety promotion.

Now, we have people wondering if cataracts and lower back strain are connected to new office equipment with visual screens which may have been poorly designed. Now we worry as well about inadequate attention to human factors, inadequate attention to ergonomics. Now we have people worrying about exposure to dioxin at work, worrying about the lingering effects of a variety of possibile carcinogens at work.

Given 10 and 11 percent unemployment, newly-glimpsed health and safety concerns temporarily diminish. But these concerns will rise again because they are well-grounded. Dramatic new reports will continue to appear indicating that so many men who previously were working in such-and-such an industry failed to achieve their actuarial life expectancy by such-and-such a percent. And *The National Enquirer,* the best selling tabloid in America, will pick up this report and help spread an exaggerated, flamboyant, pulse-racing sense of this or that new health and safety risk at work. There is great doubt in white collar as well as blue collar workplaces—in offices as well as plants, warehouses, truck terminals, and loading docks—great doubt that the well-being of the average American is being given all the attention and all the care that America would like to think it should get.

Turning back to my crystal ball, I expect more attention to the stressors we know as de-skillinization. Part of our attendance here at this conference has to do with our sense of professionalism, has to do with our desire to stay up on things, our sense of the pleasure we take in being current, in staying abreast of developments. That's a very invigorating skill. De-skillinization, in contrast, would entail cancelling this conference series—announcing that this is the last one, there will be no more conferences because we do not have to keep up our grasp of this most moving subject. You will be sent videotapes of everything you need to know about mental health and industry, and be asked to schedule a 20-minute private screening for yourself once every 12 months. A selected videotape will do it all. You will not experience hallway dialogue, you will not exchange ideas at lunch, you will not get to know one another. In this way, we would continue to dilute your sense of what's appropriate to your professionalism.

This story of de-skillinization is occurring across the American labor force. If you talk as I do with members of the Amalgamated Butchers Workers—they've merged recently with the United Food and Commercial Workers, and are now perhaps the largest union in the country, depending on how seriously you take Teamster Union claims—these butchers used to be stiletto artists. Years ago they really worked the meat behind the supermarket glass sliding wall. They do not do this any longer. Now, they merely warehouse meat. And their wage rates, skill levels, and pride all reflect their loss of skills. What they do with meat now is handle it the way industry handles manufacturing. And you're familiar with that.

Are you familiar with the fact that men and women who used to do internal repair for the phone company, literally move around a vast and complex phone service building all day, do not do that anymore? Instead, they take phone complaints and then, in that incredibly electronic computerized maze, watch while electronic robots now handle the problems. Similarly, when industry containerized the Brooklyn docks, workers were guaranteed lifetime earnings if they lost work. So, at 5:30 every morning, hundreds of men assembled on the Brooklyn docks to punch in, only to be told at 7 a.m. that which they knew beforehand, namely, that there is no work for them. But they have to get paid. And then they have a deskilled day to fill.

The third crystal ball item of job strain is what I call the erosion of institutional support. Now what does that mean? It means the National Labor Relations Board has fewer people than ever working for it. Now, why is that relevant to industrial mental health? Because it takes longer today than at any time in the history of the NLRB to get justice. Indeed, it takes so long that workers find it hard to remember what their grievance was all about. The Constitution promises people the swift handling of their legal problems. We have a statute of limitations. But the NLRB does not have a statute of limitations. You get your case brought to the NLRB and it can languish there. You only *go* to the NLRB because your grievance is important. As it is important, it deserves appropriate and swift attention. It does not get that when an organization is increasingly reduced in staffing and related resources.

Another example of erosion of institutional support

involves the American trade movement. The AFL-CIO this year will institute a 10 percent across-the-budget cut—that means pink-slipping. The United Steelworkers Union is pink-slipping many on its staff. (The United Steelworkers Union in 1980-81 had 1.4 million dues-paying members. It now has under 800,000 and is falling.)

The 108 unions in the AFL-CIO, and other unions as well, have taken a shellacking in the recession, and the recovery will reach them only slowly. They expect further contraction in their financial resources, in their personal power, and in their bargaining power. In this recent recession, working men and women turned to their labor organizations and said, "What can you do for us?" And the answer was, "Very, very little. We'll cut the best deal we can." Now, everybody understands that, but you've got to understand its pathos to fully appreciate it.

I would leave you with this last statistic: the AP-NBC poll in 1978 asked the American public, among other things, how many of you expect that your children will have a higher standard of living? In 1978, more than a third of the American public thought their youngsters would have a higher standard of living. Now, you appreciate how important is this sort of displaced aspiration. You appreciate how important is upward mobility. You appreciate how important is this inter-generational dream. America is a bootstrap, Ellis Island culture where we all like to think our children are going to have a higher-than-ever standard of living. But when the NBC poll repeated the question in 1983, the figure was different, *much* different. It had fallen to eight percent.

To understand America in 1983, and to understand mental health and industry, and to understand the challenge that we have at a conference like this, is to understand a nagging suspicion that this advanced industrial nation is no longer on top of events, but is being buffeted instead by events. It is to grasp the public's suspicion that this advanced industrial nation is making decisions at the macro level—political and economic—that have caused human casualties in every imaginable direction: those out of work, those nervous about when they might lose work, those children who no longer have community mill towns and the factory as a fallback.

My steelworker friends were always ambivalent about their sons, and perhaps their daughters, going into the mill. Always ambivalent. That's why we created the community college movement in this country. That's why we put Penn State branches out in Braddock and Johnstown.

But what was critical was that the mill was a fallback, it was there. Their fathers had worked it, they were now working it themselves, they were proud, they were macho, they were men. All of that is threatened, disappearing, or gone. We've banked the furnaces and, in the process, we have dampened hope. Their hope is growing cold, and so their problems reach very deep.

I sense the burden this places on all of us, but I've come to the conference trusting in our seriousness about this challenge. And, of course, nobody ever promised us a rose garden...not the workers, their employers, or those of us who can and must help *both* sides gain better mental health at and away from work.

SELECTED READING

Albrecht, Karl, *Stress and the Manager: Making It Work For You,* Englewood Cliffs, N.J.: Prentice-Hall (Spextrum), 1979

Cooper, C.L. and Payne, R., Eds., *Stress at Work* New York: John Wiley & Sons, 1978

Ferman, Louis A., and Gordus, Jeanne P., Eds., *Mental Health and the Economy*, Kalamazoo, Mich.: W.E. Upjohn, 1979

House, James S., *Occupational Stress and the Mental and Physical Health of Factory Workers*, Ann Arbor, Mich.: Survey Research Center, 1980

Shostak, Arthur B., *Blue Collar Stress*, Reading, Mass.: Addison-Wesley, 1980

DISCUSSION

Chaired by speaker Dr. Shostak, this panel included: Fred B. Charatan, M.D., Clinical Director, South Oaks Hospital; Norman Goodman, Ph.D., Professor and Chairman, Department of Sociology, State University of New York at Stony Brook; Henry J. Kraeter, M.P.S., Director of Personnel, South Oaks Hospital; and Graham Spanier, Ph.D., Vice Provost and Professor of Sociology and Psychiatry, State University of New York at Stony Brook.

Dr. Charatan:
The problem of unemployment is clearly a major one, preoccupying our political leaders and also those of us in the mental health field. As Dr. Shostak pointed out, the high level of unemployment is statistically linked with a greater incidence of emotional disorders, family conflict, violence, crimes, suicide, and a high mortality rate. Dr. Shostak described for us some of the responses to the problem of unemployment, the need for retraining, and the job-a-thon which some people might well characterize as being a Band-Aid on a really malignant process.

It's always seemed to me that the price of unemployment, even if it's not borne directly by a corporation which has to cut back on the number of people it employs, is borne by the larger society; and the way it's borne is very familiar to all of you, in terms of the emotional disorders I've just referred to, and also the economic losses because of the need for the government to pay out unemployment benefits, the fall in tax revenues, and so forth.

Dr. Shostak concluded with a somewhat pessimistic view of future expectations of workers today, that their children will not have as high a standard of living as they themselves have had, and fewer expect their children to live more affluently. So that, as we can all see, the mental health problems of the unemployed do affect us all, and really challenge us to find ways to deal with them.

Dr. Spanier:

I'm a newcomer to New York State, and shortly after my arrival at SUNY Stony Brook, I learned that the state has some very unusual ways of doing business when it comes to dealing with the issues of employment and unemployment. Specifically, a new state budget had been proposed by the governor which would eliminate 14,000 state jobs—a good number of them on Long Island, and 400 to 500 of them at SUNY Stony Brook. This budget was just a proposal; the state legislature could take up to one month to review the proposals and rule on the budget. While the legislature was looking over the fate of several hundred of our employees, we—the university administration—were faced with the task of making up a hit-list, identifying 400 or 500 people who were to be notified within a month that they had lost their jobs if the legislature approved the governor's budget.

I think we were very wise in keeping the hit-list private, because it turned out that the budget was changed drastically by the legislature and the state jobs were kept intact. In some locations across the state, however, state agencies notified their employees that a certain number were to lose their jobs—in fact, some people even received layoff notices, which were subsequently rescinded. Imagine the job jitters in a situation like that. Imagine the strain on employees.

I think we tend to look at issues surrounding employment and unemployment in one of two extreme ways. We tend to look at them very globally in terms of the nightly news unemployment statistics; that's sort of a very general impression of what's going on in the country, and we can look at that very philosophically. Or we tend to look at it very individually—when a particular person who was laid off and is out of work is featured. But the implications of the whole range of issues concerning unemployment—the ripple effect of job strain and job jitters for everyone—are also very important in that range in between the idividual who was laid off and the unemployment rate in the country as a whole.

I think we don't even know the degree to which the whole range of issues concerning unemployment permeates our lives. I think they do so even more so than we might expect.

I'd also like to comment on some of the family consequences of dual-career couples. I've done quite a bit of marriage and family therapy, and over the past 10 years I've seen a dramatic increase in the kinds of cases that relate to male-female issues and a subset of those issues, which is very often dual-worker problems.

What happens when one of the two partners loses his or her job? That raises some interesting issues as to the effects on the family, the dynamics of the marital relationship. Virtually all women in the United States work outside the home sometime in their adult lives and, at any given time, slightly over half of all married women are in the labor force. The single greatest category contributing to the overall increase in women in the labor force in the last few years is women with young children.

It now is typical for a husband and wife both to be working or seeking work. Loss of the job for the husband or the wife raises important questions regarding self-esteem, particularly among professional men and women. What does it mean for one member of the couple to be out of work when they're both used to working? How does that affect their self-esteem and how does that self-esteem affect their relationship? We know that when husbands and wives both work, there is a feeling of independence. For one of them to now be out of work means that, at least financially, they are completely dependent on the other person.

One of the big issues when one person is out of work is having to redefine the allocation of household tasks. Most working couples have arrived at some kind of division of labor, and now with one person out of work, they have to re-think who does the cooking, who handles the laundry, and who cleans up the house.

In short, there are a range of interpersonal and marital issues that develop in a situation like that that are different from the ones we would normally think about in relation to unemployment.

As for the balance of commitment between work and family, in terms of actual hours in a given day there can be no equality of statement of home versus family commitment. Most people work eight hours a day, and there's time getting ready for work, travelling to work, coming back from work, and unwinding from work. For the typical working person, that day is centered around work. Our days are filled with our work. There's very little time left over for family activities. So the whole question of work versus family commitments is an important one, because it's not just a matter of saying, "What are my priorities, and what do I really want to do with my life?" If you are a working person, you have a built-in set of commitments and restrictions on your time that, no matter how high your priority is for your family, are going to make your life complicated.

Dr. Goodman:

I think the issue of working families has become a major public concern in our country only over the last decade or two. Before that, you had essentially a traditional family structure and set of cultural supports for a traditional family. The man worked, the woman's work was at home, and the man, if he was nice, helped out. If he was not nice, he sat by like a king and let his wife do all the work. The issue of adjusting family and work responsibilities was really a question of how could the wife adjust her schedule around the husband's needs. That's not the case anymore in most families.

Dr. Spanier talked about the kinds of problems that therapists and counselors now see that essentially are problems in role relationships, and I would submit that that's really the tip of the iceberg. The bulk of us struggle through on a day-to-day basis, without seeking professional help, with those problems of dual jobs, the adjustment of work and family responsibilities. the reshaping of our sense of what it means to be a husband and wife, a mother, a father, from what we learned when we grew up, to what we now understand it should be, or what other people think it should be.

There's a whole set of skills that have to go along with the cultural changes affecting men and women's roles. We have not really come to grips with understanding what they are and how we can train people to develop these skills. And that deficiency in our training carries over into problems not only in the home, but in the workplace, too.

We've heard that there have been seven recessions since 1945. Why is it worse now? It's worse now because most workers increasingly believe that this is a *structural* change. As Art Shostak said, they believe that they're not likely to get their jobs back, or anything remotely like it. It isn't, "I'll be out of work for a couple of weeks and don't worry I've got enough to tide me over," but, "I will never get back to doing the thing that I've been trained to do, that I spent time doing, that I've committed myself to doing, and that I want to do."

It's living with that, having to face up to that, that makes this recession distinctly different. The structural change in the American economic system means the feeling of powerlessness is only going to increase, the sense of anxiety and dread are only going to increase, and the consequences for physical and mental health will also increase.

Mr. Kraeter:

I'd like to comment on employee assistance programs—how we can support, help, heal the employee or the family. How much responsibility does management have toward employees—from cradle to grave? Where do you draw the line? At South Oaks, we provide patient care but also care for our employees. The question is how does an employee not become a patient? We answered the question by setting up an employee assistance program.

These programs work. We often don't know how much the employee or the employee's family has been assisted by these programs, but we help with the first step, assisting the individual to make the first step toward getting help.

Sometimes that's the hardest step. If an employee is having a problem—let's say with a question of a divorce, or an adoption—it's important that the employee know the agencies out there to contact for help. That's a beginning.

And often, the individual needs that support. The EAP helps the individual take that first step.

We have had employees who were helped, and our productivity naturally increased. Our services to our patients improved. We feel that the money the EAP costs us is well worth the advantages to our employees.

As for families of employees, our EAP is open to families. The wife of an employee can call us if she's having problems with her child in school. The problem may have nothing to do with the workplace, but we'll help. Because families are important to the mental health of our employees.

Audience:

I'm director of the mental health units of a county probation department. People won't stay powerless for long; it's such a painful feeling. Everybody has to have a sense of mastery. Working with people who come into the criminal justice system, I see a lot of acting-out by youngsters and by unemployed people. People who are feeling powerless to function in socially accepted ways, get a sense of having put something over when they act in socially unacceptable ways. I think one of the emerging issues in joblessness and job jitters is a desire to find status elsewhere other than in the usual legitimate opportunity system.

Dr. Goodman:

That's one form of response to powerlessness, and in the probation department you see those who have chosen that route. Another form is obviously the kind of physical and psychiatric disorders we're talking about here.

Even more pragmatically, most of us, I think, have learned by experience not to buy a car made on a Monday or a Friday. And I think that's related to the point that you're making; when you're powerless, you really do look for ways in which you can have some effect upon the world. We've learned, at least in some industries like the auto industry, the one way you do that is by not doing what you're told you should be doing.

Dr. Charatan:

Dr. Shostak referred to the increasing aging of the population and, of course, with age, as one well knows, a sense of powerlessness can very much increase. It's no accident that retirement can pose serious problems for white middle-class men who identify strongly with work. It's no accident that the suicide rate for the older white male population is three or four times the national average. I think that's linked very much with loss of job and powerlessness.

Audience:

I'm a firm advocate of employee counseling services; however, a question that hasn't been addressed is, how long do you permit a worker to continue with counseling? For instance, in our firm we have an alcoholic who has been in and out of the program for the last seven years. He has delusions; he has called the police in claiming that there were people with drawn guns in the building. How long does an employer suffer with a person like this?

Mr. Kraeter:

With an alcoholic employee, you know you are not getting 100 percent; you may be down to 50 percent. You must demand good work performance and set time limits. You may be bending over backwards for this employee, but you must delineate a point that you can't go beyond. It's a progressive discipline of saying to the individual, "Put your life together and take care of your problem, and we'll

help, but you've got to work." Then decide on a time se-
quence. Six months? A year? You are then putting that
employee on notice that his job is in jeopardy. You are
saying, "I will work with you, but you have to help. We will
give you one month, three months—whatever the time limit
is—to turn around. I am expecting this to happen." And
then work with the individual. It's a question of the hard
line approach; "We've given you these opportunities, you
still have not turned it around, and we have to separate
you from our employment." That's the tough line.

Dr. Charatan:

I think there comes a point in an employee's working
life when he crosses the boundary from the working role
to the sick role. The alcoholic employee who has delusions
or hallucinations that people are going to attack him has
clearly crossed that line. I think it's a task of clinical judge-
ment of a good psychiatrist to consult with you when the
employee has passed that line.

Audience:

I'm a clinical social worker and a counselor for an employee assistance program. I think training is very important. If you don't train your supervisors how to refer early
on, if you don't train your union delegate how to refer
early on, you're going to be dealing with the employee who
has presented a chronic problem for many years. You're
going to be dealing with the supervisor who turns the other
cheek, and covers up and doesn't want to deal with the
situation. You are going to deal with the delegate who feels
that he has to support this employee even though he's a
dysfunctional employee. Training is a very important
component of any EAP program.

Audience:

In talking about the ripple effects of today's economy, a population you haven't mentioned is the young person about to enter the world of work. When I went to college in the mid-60's, school was still school. When I talk to students in college today, school is very definitely work, and those kids are much more concerned than my peers were about what will happen to them when they graduate.

Dr. Spanier:

You're identifying what has become a real dilemma for university administrators, because universities are now under intense pressure by students and their families to design curricula in such a way that students will be immediately employable when they graduate. This has always been the way it is in fields like engineering and agriculture, but when you talk about the large area of arts and sciences, that's where the dilemma comes in.

As the person responsible for acting on student petitions at our university, with 12,000 undergraduates, I have the final say, so to speak, as to whether or not a student is allowed to graduate with something that's different from what the faculty said they wanted the student to graduate with. Virtually all the petititons now focus on employability after graduation.

Thinking of myself as an educator first, I would wish these petitions would give some educational reason why students think they should graduate without this course, or without that requirement. But the reason is almost always "I have a job offer and I have loans to pay off," and "If I don't have my degree on this date, I won't get that job." The theme that shows up in their statements as to why the university must grant them variations is very money-oriented and career-oriented. Of course, it puts us in a real dilemma because, most of the time, they've got a good point from a practical standpoint about what's happening in their lives. But they don't have a good point at all in terms of what an educated person with a bachelor's degree ought to have.

Audience:

   As a volunteer at a crisis intervention center, I deal with people who are suicidal, who are depressed, who beat their wives, and children, and who use drugs and alcohol. These are symptoms of the feeling of powerlessness. Many of these people are working, but they are underemployed. Even though they're working, they still cannot pay the bills. So they begin to act out this powerlessness by attacking those closest to them. I believe our real problem is a moral problem—basically, the problem of greed. There is enough wealth in the world, but there are too many people who are consumed by greed.

Dr. Charatan:

   Most problems of the kind you mentioned—drug abuse, alcohol, wife-beating—I think can be justly regarded as symptoms of some kind of conflict within the individual. The symptoms, of course, can be generated, as you've well pointed out, by powerlessness due to underemployment, and forces that prevent one from becoming an adequate provider. However, I wonder whether a total redistribution of wealth, which is a political solution, would really solve all these problems. I've always felt that the person who is greedy, who is unwilling to give, has in some way failed to achieve complete human maturity. So I regard the problem of greed, of egotism, as being an infantile kind of fixation, some failure to grow and mature. Because a mature person can give, and gets gratification from giving. The question is enormously complex and a simple answer cannot be given.

Dr. Goodman:

I'd like to comment from a sociological point of view. If we redistribute wealth, and we take those people that we define as greedy and somehow through some moral or psychiatric education program, work them over, so to speak, I think we'll find in a short period of time, a new maldistribution of wealth, a new set of individuals to take their place. This is so because I believe that there are certain consequences built into the very structure of our economic system. That is not to say those are all bad. There are trade-offs. You gain certain advantages from the system we have, and you lose certain advantages. The question is, what kind of structural changes can we make that will reduce the negative side of the trade-off and increase the positive side?

Audience:

In the last six years I've gone through three terms of unemployment. Although at one time certain groups were on unemployment lines, what we're seeing now is the 60's generation who became professional career people and who now find themselves out of employment. When you compete for jobs where there are 250 applicants for one job, when you go on interview after interview, the emotional and psychological impact is very frightening.

When you lose self-esteem, you become so alienated and depressed that you'd rather go into a bar and talk to strangers than talk to somebody who's close to you.

And, when you are employed again, no matter where it is, and how much security you feel you have, your way of looking at perhaps bucking the system is quite different.

Audience:

I guess you might say I'm voluntarily unemployed, but it's funny how many of the feelings I have are similar to the people who were laid off or fired. I resigned from a state job six months ago, and I just assumed eventually I would get a job. But I haven't gotten a job, and I find myself thinking that maybe I will not get a job. It's very hard to accept that. I'm a professional, so I still have my profession, but do I if I don't do it?

One feels as though one is really alone, and that's one of the things we have to struggle against. We have to find ways to help people who are going through this, who may have to make really great changes. The steelworkers may never make steel again; they must find other ways to find real meaning. They have to find work and money, but they have to find other meanings, too, that cannot be wiped out by external forces.

Dr. Goodman:

Here's precisely the point in which the psychiatric views and the sociological views need to come together. On one hand, there needs to be provided the kind of support you talk about to reduce the isolation and to deal with the kinds of problems that real, live, flesh-and-blood individuals have in this circumstance. At the same time, unless those people in their collective wisdom begin to focus on the structural changes that are necessary to reduce the problem for themselves and for others, for now and for the future, all we'll be doing is proliferating support groups. We must locate the sources of the problem that need to be worked on. Certainly support groups are essential, but action groups are even more essential.

Dr. Spanier:

Realistically, most of the people we're talking about are the least likely to have access to mental health services where somebody could help them put their problems in perspective. In my mind, the only realistic opportunity that these people have for something to be done on their behalf is as they're leaving the organization. I think most organizations are not really disposed to do anything more than a token effort in that direction. And once people are unemployed and they don't have the support structure they were a part of, then they really are out. They're all by themselves, and where do they go? We really have lost them at that point. I think we have to turn to the government to provide some leadership, and the proper funding, to address some way of helping organizations to provide services.

It certainly wouldn't have to be the government if industry was able and willing to do it, but I just don't think that's very realistic.

Dr. Shostak:

I'd like to mention the book *In Search of Excellence*, written by Tom Peters and Robert Waterhouse, Jr., two professional students of corporate life who teach graduate business courses. The book focuses in depth on something like 65 major American companies that meet the criteria of financial success—they have a good return on investment. More important, the companies are regarded by large numbers of their employees as excellent places to work. We can extract from the book some insights quite relevant to what I think we've been talking about.

For example, Hewlett-Packard tries not to lay off anyone. IBM hasn't laid off anyone they claim, in the 34 years since the company was founded. At Hewlett-Packard everybody took a 20 percent cut, from the heads of the company on down, in order to protect the cash-flow position of the company and to share the plight. Both management and labor agreed to take a reduction in their standard of living in order to keep their fellow human beings from being on the jobless hit-list. It was a dramatic demonstration of the widest good for the widest number.

Now, wouldn't it have been interesting if everybody at SUNY Stony Brook—the faculty, staff, cleaning people—had said they would take a reduction in their standard of living in order to keep their fellow human beings from the hit-list. That would have been a dramatic demonstration of community. That would have been exemplary of the academic institution's highest ideals. That would have been "communal" in the old-fashioned sense of the widest good for the widest number.

Dr. Goodman:
A number of the faculty suggested precisely that, but the union said no. The argument essentially was that we were not going to affect the 90 percent of our membership that would be remaining on the job to save the 10 percent who might be cut.

Mr. Kraeter:
There was another instance where 15 employees were going to be laid off from a nursing home. It got to where management said, we have to reduce and if we reduce down the line, we can save these 15 jobs. But they couldn't get the union to cooperate.

Dr. Spanier:
I think we all know of examples where union employees won't budge, or cooperate. They take the position that there is, in a sense, a bottomless pot of money out there. But, in recent cases that we've seen in the automobile industry, in Hewlett-Packard, and so on, there isn't a bottomless pot. The corporation knows what the bottom line is, and at some point, and in some cases, the workers finally do become convinced that it's not just a labor-management game, but there really is a problem, and they know a lot of people are going to be in very big trouble.

Dr. Shostak:

The 65 outstanding companies profiled in *In Search of Excellence* believe in full disclosure, full information. They tell all. And they tell all *all* the time, and by doing that, they create and continue to build a climate of trust.

Dr. Spanier:

I think most of those companies over the long run have been very successful, and have had profit-sharing plans and employee stock options, where the employees have seen some of the benefits of the success of those companies, and so, psychologically, have much more of an investment in it.

Dr. Goodman:

Commitment, the identification with the institution, with the organization, with the company, is essential. If that commitment is built on a relationship of trust, which is what you are talking about, then you can weather all kinds of storms. In many respects it's like a good marriage—marriages have to face all kinds of storms, and they face them better when there's a sense of trust that's been built up, and a sense of openness. Then, when immediate decisions have to be made or actions taken without discussion, they can be accommodated, they can be tolerated, they can be accepted because of the backlog of trust. But only if you have that backlog first.

Dr. Charatan:

Well, I can go back much earlier than marriage. I'd say that the corporation that is open, has full disclosure, and promotes the atmosphere of trust, is really replicating what is essential for a "normal personality"—the early infantile sense of trust.

Dr. Shostak:

Let me add just a couple of things. The successful companies nurture risk-taking and they view employees with the terminology that the Japanese-managed American-based companies are now using. Language is always revealing. Employees are not employees, they're "associates." The associates have human capital. There's endless return on well-nurtured human capital. So it isn't a matter of demanding that our employees perform to get our 100 percent from them. That's a very stressful point of view. That is, I think, a bad parent-unruly child setting. Instead, these 65 eminently successful companies are *fun* to work *with*, not for. Hewlett-Packard is a way of life. Much of IBM is a way of thinking and being. Now it isn't Utopia; they do have problems, and they'll talk to you about their problems. They're working on their problems. Their problems are not in the closet with the door kept closed. Their problems are sensitively addressed. So the word "fun" comes up, again and again.

Audience:

I think the thing that's so discouraging is our penchant in this country for the quick fix. What happened at Hewlett-Packard didn't happen overnight. And I think where the Hewlett-Packards have been successful was that they really embarked some years ago on a long-range planning program, and they've let the thing develop with a conscious plan in mind. And if there were some failures along the way, so be it. They are committed, as a matter of policy, to a much larger development scope. But many companies give a project six months, a year, and if it doesn't work, it's no good.

Unless we stop looking for quick answers, and unless we think in terms of long-range goals, we're going to be on a negative downslide for a long time to come.

Dr. Shostak:

We've had no measurable increase in productivity in this country for four to five years, though we don't measure productivity very well, so it's hard to know what that means. We still have the most productive labor force in the world. It still takes the average American worker less time to earn a loaf of bread than any other worker anywhere. And there's a residual of pride in the American work force. A residual. It's in trouble, but there's still pride there. There is Yankee know-how, there are Rube Goldberg machines at work, there are workers that save companies and employers by adapting. We ought not to lose sight of that. There is a substantial reservoir of talent.

Dr. Goodman:

The whole structure of the economy in this country is such that it forces managers to look at short-term rather than long-term goals. And the consequence of that is not to take advantage of the reservoir of talent available.

Companies lose the value of being able to tolerate what are, in any program, the inevitable short-term defeats and negative consequences, even if the long-term consequences are likely to be very good. It's easier to say than to do, but we need to really look beyond the immediate future in order to make the immediate future better than it is likely to be if we don't.

Chapter 2

WHAT ORGANIZATIONS CAN AND MUST DO TO IMPROVE THE MENTAL HEALTH OF EMPLOYEES

Howard Hess, M.D.

Dr. Art Shostak talked about the vast unhappiness created by joblessness. I, too, see vast unhappiness but from a somewhat different standpoint. My work is 100 percent with employees who are working, many of them being well-paid, some being over-paid, many having jobs for life. And yet, they're still unhappy on the job. Frequently they're not terribly productive. And that I think is one of the reasons we got to the position we are today in terms of unem-

Howard Hess received his M.D. degree at Washington University in St. Louis in 1952. A graduate of the Psychoanalytic Institute of the Columbia University College of Physicians and Surgeons, Dr. Hess is a Diplomate of the American Board of Psychiatry and Neurology [Psychiatry]. His interest in occupational psychiatry began in the early 60's as a consultant to the Peace Corps. He has been the Staff Psychiatrist to *The New York Times* and is currently the Agency Psychiatrist for The Port Authority of New York and New Jersey and the Corporate Psychiatrist of the newly formed AT & T (formerly the Western Electric Company.) Dr. Hess has published many articles on occupational psychiatry in both business and medical journals.

ployment. We have somehow managed our work force in such a way that we have great unhappiness, great alienation, and tremendous amount of silence in the way people manage. What can industry do? What can the worker do?

Let's start with industry. Most of us when thinking about the mental health of employees, always think of what the company can do for us. And obviously the company can do more than the employee can do to manage the company in today's environment. What can the company do? The company can communicate better. I can hear you saying, "This guy comes here to tell me the company can communicate better?" Yes, that's what I mean.

When I'm called in as a consultant to an ailing department, an ailing work group, an ailing warehouse, I usually find that the workers there are very much alienated from their company and from their supervisors. They simply don't feel a part of the organization. Many times their work life descends to a level in which some of their greatest kicks come from sabotaging the company they work for. One toll collector on a bridge in New York told me her greatest joy in coming to work is that every day gives her the unexcelled possibility of screwing management. Every day, she had that possibility, and that was her fulfillment in coming to work. That's not the kind of communication I'm talking about.

I find the same things that I learned clinically as a psychiatrist in private practice also occur on the factory floor. Much of the kinds of disorganization and silence that produce unhappy families produce unhappy workers and unhappy management.

Let me give you a few clinical examples. I once treated a family in which the mother had a strange disease, not really strange, but strange insofar as this upper middle class family was concerned. Mom was an alcoholic. Everyone in this family acted as if mother were a normal member of society and she was not. The fact of mother's alcoholism was never discussed, was never made part of the family process and planning and general communication. Living that lie obviously produced major difficulties within that family.

Let me give you another example. I treated a family of two daughters, a son, mommy and daddy which was not your typical American family in one respect. Daddy had a mistress and approximately three nights a week he was out of the family household. Once again, for their own reasons, the family treated this as if they were living in a normal atmosphere. The son who was the youngest didn't want to see his father that way, and the daughters really got into a conspiracy with their mother to protect her. Everyone in the family knew what was going on. The simple opening up of the fact, with the entire family together, that Daddy was living this strange life and had no desire to change it, and that the family had no desire to change it, and that the family had no desire to have him leave the family, made for a much less sick family environment. In other words, open communication does a great deal for mental health.

In industry, several years ago, I was called in as a consultant to the management of a huge warehouse in the eastern panhandle of West Virginia. The warehouse had been open four years when I arrived there to try to ascertain why so many of the employees were having severe accidents. Several months before I arrived, a young man had fallen 11 feet from a forklift truck to a cement floor. This young guy had a very hard head. He fractured his skull, but survived. He was approximately the eighth person—this is in a work group of 100—to have a severe accident in the past two years. This warehouse was part of a company that employed well over 100,000 people. The accident rate at the warehouse was by far the highest in the entire corporation. Orthopedic surgeons in this town were getting rich fixing backs being hurt on the factory floor.

And when I came in, I found a very interesting situation—truly a group of alienated employees. The warehouse was in a rural town, and approximately 10 years before this warehouse was built, industry began to exploit the area. But almost all the people employed there were farm children. They grew up on farms; farming was their work life. That was what they knew. Suddenly they were thrown into an industrial setting, with fancy automated machinery, and who was leading them? Who did this big company choose to supervise? Traditional big company supervisors are college-educated kids from big towns; from Washington, from St. Louis, two from Cleveland, Ohio. Not one person on the supervisory force was a local hire. The supervisors essentially looked down upon the hillbilly work force. The work force mistrusted the city slickers, college-educated young professional managers. As one young man who had just had his back operated on said, "Doctor, I can take you out on that warehouse floor and in five minutes, I'll show you 10 safety violations. Now if I can see them, why can't the supervisors?" And true to his word, he did that. And certainly these college-educated supervisors could see them. They were somewhat frightened of this rural work force and they did nothing or very little to enforce safety regulations.

What we did was institute a committee of workers elected by the workers to work on warehouse problems. The committee has just had their 150th meeting which is a long time for a committee to work in industry. A year after the committee was formed, the accident rate fell to zero. For two years in a row, they've won the safety award for that region of the company. But more than that, they are beginning to work much more effectively with their supervisors.

We did a little test on supervisory style before and after we instituted this program; and we find that the supervisors are much more participatory after living with the program for now going on three years than they were before it began. There is a closeness, the alienation is gone, people are performing better, and the warehouse is getting new manufacturing work.

In a plant located in a large industrial city in the northeast, I was called to see a group of 15 employees working in a die laboratory. This little lab, with only 15 employees, was a rather important place. The first industrial laser ever used in the world was broken in by these workers. The laser cut diamonds. These people's task was to constantly cut and polish diamonds when they became worn in cable-making. The lab had 2 men, 13 women and was a microcosm of blue collar America. Their only problem was that they did not know how to make diamond dies. Whenever I deal with engineers and supervisors, I find a similar set of misconceptions. Management always feels that workers know how to do something and are not doing it because they are lazy, ineffective, rip-off artists. Workers frequently do not know a process but honestly believe that they know how to do something. When a committee of workers was set up to meet with engineers and management, they all began to realize their lack of knowledge concerning the job itself. The engineers spent a lot of time and effort producing a new training program. The workers were interested in being retrained because they felt that they had prodded management and engineering into making the program. It was now their program. They began to make excellent dies. Their absenteeism rate went down and for many months they actually worked without a supervisor.

Once in a large factory, I saw management and engineering move a job from a very new modern facility to an old facility. The move was made in two stages. In the first move engineering and management made all the decisions about how the move should be made and where the machinery would be placed in the new area. When that was done, production fell by almost one-half during the first several weeks in the new area. When the second group was moved, a committee of workers was allowed to participate with management and engineering in planning the move. When that was done, they actually bettered their production during the first week on the job.

The toll collector I told you about earlier, the one who was fulfilled by screwing management, worked with many other toll collectors at a giant bridge. Recently, new toll booths were built for these toll collectors. One would assume that no one in the world knows more about what would be a good environment for collecting tolls than an experienced toll collector. Possibly you will find it hard to believe that the engineers designed the new toll booths by observing toll collectors but never truly interviewed them in order to learn from their expertise. Multiply this again and again all over America and you arrive at a better idea of why Japanese workers who are consulted in the workplace are destroying us in the marketplace.

In terms of more traditional medical things that industry can do to help workers, an active alcoholism program is a necessity. Every work facility in America of any size should have an alcoholism advisor on staff. In a large organization, this can be a full-time employee. In a smaller work place, it can be a recovered alcoholic who has other duties as well. When these people are in place, it is necessary to educate your supervisors to report alcoholics to the alcohol advisor as soon as possible. I am beginning to see too many programs getting started in industry with fancy hot lines and open telephone lines that alcoholics are expected to call. I do not think in my 20 years of experience as an occupational psychiatrist that I have seen more than five alcoholics who have submitted themselves for rehabilitation. Unless supervisors do their job of finding people with poor performance who may have alcohol problems, it is simply not done.

Employee Assistance Programs are another more traditional route that seems to be catching on in America. Employee Assistance Programs do not solve the major problem in American industry which is a lack of participation on the part of the workers. But at least it allows people who are having problems off the job to work more effectively by having a place to go when they are in trouble.

What can we as employees do to help our work lives? Is there anything we can do or should we keep expecting organizations to change things? One thing workers must do is make their voices known. You say, "Well, that may get you fired." Unfortunately, many workers are so alienated that they are not even willing to share positive feelings with their organization. If the big bosses do something you like, let them know about it. If you let people know what you like, you can also let them know what you don't like; and people rarely get fired by telling someone that they did a good job.

It is good to trust your leaders, but not to trust them too much. Remember, it was not leaders who extricated us from Vietnam—it was the people. If young people were willing to make their voices known when it might have led to having to leave the country or go to prison, is it too much to ask that young people make their voices known in industry? I have given many examples today of how participation helps morale and productivity. Truly, you can paper the walls with such examples, and yet organizations do not seem to change.

Let me go over again and summarize some of the things industry might do to enhance the mental health of their employees.

1. Openness of communication—and that includes bad news.
2. Workers need communication committees and participation.
3. There is a need for the coaching of supervisors so they can do better with employees. Most evaluations of supervisors go on paper. The development of supervisors who develop employees has never been high on the agenda of American industry.
4. Ask the advice of workers more. Someone who does a job for a long time knows a lot about that job and might be able to improve it.
5. When workers can't get something right, don't automatically assume that they are lazy. They may need knowledge more than kicks.
6. Set up alcoholism programs which are high on educating supervisors about alcoholism and finding alcoholics.
7. Employee Assistance Programs are worth more than they cost. Troubled employees do not produce well.

DISCUSSION

Chaired by speaker Dr. Hess, this panel included: Vincent J. Gallagher, M.D., Associate Medical Director, Grumman Aerospace Corporation; Hagop S. Mashikian, M.D., Senior Psychiatrist, South Oaks Hospital; Anne Nelson, Co-Director, Institute on Women and Work, New York State School of Industrial and Labor Relations, Cornell University; and Howard A. Van Jones, Recording Secretary, Local 504, Transport Workers Union, and Director of Local 504's Special Health Services Committee.

Dr. Gallagher:

Within our corporation, we are on the threshold of developing more employee assistance programs. I think any organization that's worth its salt has to look further on down the road and go about developing assistance programs. We have had, over the last several years, an alcohol rehabilitation program; fortunately, it's been a very enlightened program—our success rate is close to 75 percent.

We also concurrently have other chemical substance abuse programs. We have a nationwide organization and also a worldwide organization. Oftentimes on the overseas sites, we work hand-in-hand with the United States Navy, and in some instances, with the United States Air Force. In turn, we must depend upon their assistance programs to help us out. We monitor the success and the compliance of the employee back here in New York.

We have ongoing educational programs designed to train supervisors to identify the employee who has an alcoholic problem, or problems with abuse of other chemicals. These educational programs are invaluable in helping front-line supervisors to identify the individual who has a problem, and then in turn, refer him into the medical department so we can get that individual properly treated.

There are other components of assistance programs that a lot of the large corporations have that we are looking into; for instance, financial counseling and legal counseling. We cannot only expect employees to be productive if we provide them with a safe, healthy working environment, but we should also try to put in place some of those support mechanisms off the site which can alleviate some of their distress.

Mr. Van Jones:

The question before us I find most interesting. It's not just what *can* organizations do, but what *must* organizations do. That's really dramatic, because it has to be a *must* situation. It no longer can be simply we *should* do this or we *can* do that. We must act, and we must act appropriately. For labor unions especially, we need to enhance our image. We often hear of the shoddy side of labor organizations, and they seem to be front-page news. We don't hear about the majority of honest labor organizations who provide a host of social programs as well as fair representation. For instance, the Central Labor Rehabilitation Council of New York, of which I'm a board member, in 1962, started what they called then Project Rehab. It was, and still is, funded and supported by labor unions. Our goal is to provide appropriate referrals to workers who needed rehabilitation services. They started an educational program to train shop stewards, the union leadership, and rank and file members to identify problem employees, and to intervene, motivate, and make appropriate referrals.

Since 1962, they've trained thousands of trade union counselors in the greater New York area. So we have done a lot in this field, but there's a lot more to be done. We have trained social workers, so if the trained counselor is unsure of the appropriate referral, he can turn to the Council's trained social worker to assist in the referral.

In most major cities in the country, there are city labor councils. They have different methods, perhaps. Those that can't afford their own social workers will rely heavily on United Way. And they do a great job. There's generally a liaison officer of the labor council and the United Way. Also there are interlocking relationships with health carriers such as HIP and Blue Cross/Blue Shield. These two insurance carriers, incidentally, rely on organized labor and their input.

It's essential that labor play a role with management in the best interest of the employee and the union member. But there is much more that needs to be done. Fortunately, I play two roles. I bargain collectively for my membership, I sit at negotiations, I'm generally the spokesman, in the negotiations, and I'm also director of the special health service committee for our local union. We deal with 12 to 14 companies. Some are very cooperative and we have a dual role with that management in employee assistance programs. In other companies, although we have the cooperation of management, we do it essentially alone. It works best when we can convince management that we have a joint committee.

In my role as a bargaining agent, I see the need to be more creative. Most people perceive the collective bargaining process as an adversary relationship between labor and management—you sit at this big table and everyone is smoking a cigar and fighting and trying to shake each other down. That's not the case. You generally have two parties who have one common interest, and that's to reach an agreement. We at least share that one value system.

The innovation and creativity that I see can be employed at the bargaining table would be to include the corporation's medical director and others who provide health care, including the insurance carrier. Rather than have a confrontation or an adversary relationship, we must be creative and get these people involved, get them to arrive at hard, fast statistics, to talk about preventive health care, to talk about adequate coverage.

Ms. Nelson:
I'm going to address my remarks principally to the position of women in the work force. Cornell University's Institute for Women and Work has two credit programs: one that targets trade union women to help them to par-

ticipate more actively and strongly in their locals, and another one that targets clerical women who typically are not organized except by governmental units in New York State. The clerical program has helped women move up in their jobs.

In order to help the women who are below management or professional levels, it is necessary also to activate the professional women and the management women who supervise them. You don't win by only pushing from the bottom; it also helps to have a little pull from the top. So we do conferences and workshops for government women, executive women, to remind them of their sisters below, and to ask them to bend their efforts toward helping them.

I am going to mention some of the conferences that we have conducted in order to give you a sense of where the problems of working women lie. We conducted a conference on "Mentoring" for women who are the Governor's personal appointees to state government posts. There aren't a large number of these women, but 90 percent of them came to an Albany conference where we discussed the question of mentoring: do they still have mentoring needs? Do their subordinates? You know what the term "mentor" means—to have someone to help you move up, teach you the ropes. All of us above others in work situations should be conscious of our obligation to do something like this for those people below us. At the conference, we explored this practice and it was, to me, absolutely dumbfounding. I was surprised at the depth of the obstacles confronted by these strong executive women—I am talking about commissioners and deputy commissioners—and with what they had to contend. I was surprised at the extent of the shutout they experienced from state political activity. They are in it and they are not in it. Critical discussions and critical decisions tend to be taken in informal meetings which exclude the top women.

Another conference, "Comparable Worth," focused on equal pay for work of equal value. It takes its name from the measurement and comparison of job responsibility and pay. For example, a parking lot attendant is paid more than a teacher's aide although the responsibility of a teacher's aide requires greater skill and education preparation. Workers who have jobs of comparable skill and responsibility are often paid very differently, depending on whether or not the work is in a typically male or female occupation. The female occupation is always paid less well.

The wage gap is now running better than it was, so we are making progress. It has been 59-cents to the dollar for some time. That is, the average wage of full-time working women is 59-cents for every dollar that a man earns. We are now up to about 62-cents. And in certain occupations it is very good—engineering and accounting, for example—women are being paid quite well. However, the issue of comparable worth is one that is achieving high visibility and has got to be understood by us all. Its implementation is going to be slow. It is a societal issue; it is an issue that affects both men and women. We now have 5 million women who are heads of households—and their number is growing. When a family is dependent on the women's earnings, these women have got to be earning good wages, wages that fairly remunerate them for their work.

The Institute for Women and Work had a conference recently on the subject of training minority women to be labor educators. We do not have minorities, we do not have Blacks, we do not have Hispanics—I can think of only four in the whole country—who are labor educators in universities. It is not a good scene. Since the field has been typically, and remains heavily, a male occupation, the Institute considered that it had an obligation to train Black, Hispanic, and Oriental women in the New York City headquarters. We received a grant from the Muskiwinni Foundation to train 10 minority labor union women to be labor educators. The women are sponsored by their unions and selected by a labor union committee. We have high hopes of rectifying the absence of minority women's participation in labor education.

Another activity of the Institute is conducting of brown bag lunches for the women staff members of New York City unions. We have decided to assemble a "Who's Who" directory to identify who the women staff are in New York City unions. They tend to be floating out there alone, and should know who they are and how to reach out to another staff person for advice or assistance. Labor unions are absolutely miraculous organizations who stumble occasionally, and need shoes on both feet, the male foot and the female foot. One of our missions is to try to support their efforts by bringing union staff women together, so that they have resources among each other to help with union efforts.

I think we can all see the mental health needs of union staff women. As a woman, a staff member is pretty much all alone and she often finds her position stressful. Unions have very tough problems; they've got a lot of activity, a lot of tough language, a lot of male-female interaction going on, and it's a stressful situation. There are mental health problems in these kinds of situations. And the women need support.

Now we are definitely moving ahead, but progress takes vigilance. Its rate is not rapid, but it is there. There are serious barriers in our way, however.

In the first committee report on female labor given to a national labor organization, in 1836 to the National Trades Union Convention, the committee reported: "Female labor is a physical and moral injury to women, and a competitive menace to men." Do those words awaken any echoes? I am afraid they do, but on the whole I think those sentiments have changed. We do not have such views openly expressed today. Labor's men and women have changed. The AFL-CIO now has two women on its Executive Board. It has endorsed the ERA and the comparable worth concept. There has been a vast change in labor's thinking.

One issue that I thought might interest you is the change in work concept going on for women in medical schools. It seems to me to have transfer value to many of us in other occupations. Women students enrolled in medical schools—40 percent of all medical students today are women, up from 9 percent in 1970—are being guided into what is being described as "women-appropriate" work. In the medical field, women-appropriate work is judged to be group practice, student health services, pathology, gynecology, pediatrics. Why? They have good hours. What apparently is going on in the medical schools is a discriminatory environment which directs women to areas where their commitment to a medical goal, which must be high and perfect, won't conflict with their commitment to their family role, which also must be perfect.

The mental stress that women in medicine are suffering is that the social values which underlie these two goals—commitment to medicine and commitment to family—are really in conflict. I don't know how we're going to come out of this conflict. But to commit yourself fully to a career, you've got to work very hard. The men have to, the women have to. If you really want to amount to something, you've got to be out there nights, you've got to bring work home, you've got to show up. Now how are you going to combine that with a family? For men, the answer is clear: work hard at your job. It's a very difficult question for women because of social expectations, and there are a variety of answers. But there's lots of stress in working out the right answers.

One of the issues that causes mental strain is shortage of time. All these commitments take time. But I don't believe that that is the signal problem. I think the signal problem is that the underlying moral values really are in conflict, and we're not quite sure how to straighten them out.

One interesting phenomenon among women is a complete reversal from what we have been seeing in the last 10 years. Young women often are turned off by the women's movement. They don't think they can be "superwomen," yet personal and work demands made on them are requiring almost impossible efforts from these young energetic women. They are turning aside from those demands and saying, "We want children." How many children? They are talking about only one child, or possibly two children. This is a big change. It is a voluntary lower fertility rate and it may be one of the ways we're going to solve this "superwoman" problem. There are many years left for significant career accomplishments even if childrearing is undertaken for only one or two children.

I particularly want to stress the effects of unemployment on both men and women. They are just terrible. At Cornell, we did a study of unemployment at an automobile plant that closed down. We worked with the people who were laid off. Nobody really cares much about them. The union can't afford to. When you don't have a job, you are not a full union member. That is what most unions have to practice. It is just too expensive to carry the unemployed. The unemployed people are wandering around. Guys are saying, "You know, my buddy committed suicide, and I think that he had the right idea." Their self-esteem is very seriously attacked by the loss of their jobs. These are difficult times for the women who work, whose husbands have lost their jobs. And I think we can see the problem there. Who is a man? If he hasn't got a job, he's not supporting his family, and his wife is out there at half the pay he earned. Serious problems for the working woman. She strokes her husband in his loss. But who strokes the stroker?

Dr. Mashikian:

I work clinically with patients in both management and unions. I also serve as a consultant to organizations regarding the mental health of the workers.

I have tried to link the major gaps that exist between what we know in theory, and what we deliver at the practice end. I'd like to highlight those areas, and perhaps we can discuss how organizations might and must improve the mental health of employees. I'm emphasizing the word *improve.*

I recognize that organizations are neither clinics nor hospitals, but somehow during the last 50 years, we have learned that we do have a responsibility in the general umbrella of mental health. We have learned also that that responsibility extends beyond the individual worker to the family of that worker because if an employee is under special stress, there may be one or two other victims in the family, so interaction within the family also is a concern.

Let me share with you what I have learned over the years about the difficulties employees have. Number one, oftentime a worker, who has his own expectations, comes into a big organization where, unfortunately, very few of the expectations of the organization are shared with him. His orientation to the performance and value expectations from him, by the organization, are very fluid, blurred. That blurred area contributes to stress for the employee, and it has been taken advantage of by less sensitive supervisors who may also have their own blurred visions. Unknown and blurred expectations are one area of concern in improving the mental health of the worker.

Another area. During the last 20 years, particularly during the last 14 years, many organizations have been hasty in promoting or putting minority people in certain window-dressing positions. Many of these hastily and poorly-chosen minority positions have done more disservice than service by projecting to the opponents, "You see, we told you, women, Blacks, Hispanics, cannot do the job. We gave them the top positions and they couldn't handle them, they fouled up." We do have a responsibility in being selective and making sure that through the symbolism—because many people are going to be looking at the leadership roles we are promoting—that we enhance and encourage identifications and relations that other workers are going to be developing. Failing to do that, we are going to contribute to negative forces within the employees.

When we talk about mental health, we must think along three lines. One, prevent mental illness in our employees. Two, promote the good health, or the well-being of the individual. And, three, treat the ill health and prevent the chronicity.

Unfortunately, many programs are at the level of taking care of the sick person. However, many are now anticipating the development of sickness, and therefore doing some preventive work. Discussion groups and educational programs in some industries, also have been helping to convey knowledge and information to the worker about better mental health.

Many employees are still very biased and prejudiced against mental illness. They would not want to approach their supervisors for assistance. Fortunately, more and more organizations have developed an interim group—whether it's in their medical department, or independently, the employee assistance program—where anonymity is maintained and where prejudices are bypassed. From the perception of the employee, this shows a broader and more reliable lack of prejudice against mental illness for those workers to seek help.

When employees who have experienced a breakdown in mental health return to their jobs, it is not infrequent at all for certain supervisory personnel, or peers, to make fun of them, to underscore that they're less than average, or that they are abnormal because they have been exposed to the mental health system. Something ought to be found, or done, about these very subtle eroding activities.

We have been successful recently in dealing directly with the medical departments, who are being very supportive of our efforts, but at the same time, we, in the mental health field, ought to be aware that organizations are not there primarily to promote the mental health of the employee; their bottom line is to make a profit, and run their business. But it behooves us to remind management at all levels that that employee who has been in service for several years is an expensive commodity to replace. The training and development of a new employee will cost a great deal more than what it will take to rehabilitate and treat the line employee who comes for assistance.

Audience:

In the literature about the establishment and operation of employee assistance programs, there seems to be great stress placed on getting the cooperation and support of top management, otherwise any kind of employee assistance program is going to be less than successful. I'd be interested in hearing your comments, Dr. Gallagher, on your experience with this.

Dr. Gallagher:

We're on an uphill battle, so to speak. I think Dr. Hess, in his experience, has fought a lot more battles than I have in trying to get employee assistance programs motivated through top management. Because you don't go anywhere unless they are committed to it, and thereby give you the monetary resources to start something. It's a very difficult situation. Sometimes you can't go through the front door, you have to go through the back door and that back door doesn't swing open very easily. It takes years.

Mr. Van Jones:

Where I've been successful in grabbing management's attention was to show them the cost-effectiveness of a program, to show them how much money they were actually losing by not having a program. There is a wealth of research material proving this. The National Council on Alcoholism has excellent time-proven statistics. For instance, one of the major auto manufacturers found that 48 percent of all grievances are alcohol-related; the alcohol or the substance abuser will have four times more accidents than the other employees. Obviously, it's cost effective to cut down on absenteeism, to cut down on accidents, and on and on. Studies claim that for every dollar put into a program, $12 comes back into a company. We did a research in one of our companies and it came out as a 10-to-1 ratio. For every dollar this particular company put into their program, they would get $10 back. Those statistics are out there for you.

Dr. Hess:

I have a little different experience. I find in dealing as a mental health professional and as a physician with management, especially with top management, I am much more successful in appealing to their humanitarian streak than I am to their dollar-and-cents streak. First of all, I'm on much firmer ground. They know the bottom line much better than I do. Once I get into dollars and cents with them, they can eat me alive. If I stay in my own field, which is helping people, and the need for this organization to help people, I can get to them much more directly.

In 1977, I spoke to an executive vice president and two vice presidents in Western Electric who supervised about 50,000 people in seven regions, and I was trying to get an employee assistance program for each region, with about 7,000 people in each region. I spent about 40 minutes appealing to these gentlemen and their staffs, simply on the basis of what it would do for their people. And they bought it. The bottom line was they bought it. This was a huge expenditure, and a good sell. I'm convinced if I went there with charts I would not have been so successful. Go to them where you live, not where they live. I think you may be more successful.

Mr. Van Jones:

What the doctor said is appropriate for him. He deals with health issues. I deal with money issues at the bargaining table. What works for him, works for him, and what works for me, works for me.

Audience:

What is your feeling as to whether an employee assistance program should be on-site or off-site? Often, employees are not sure of anonymity if services are on-site.

Dr. Hess:

Back in that Western Electric meeting in 1977, six of the programs turned out to be on-site, and one we referred out. We studied the groups and they're all pretty equally successful. There's been no greater use of the off-site program than the on-site. They're similar programs; all are headed by social workers, and we find very little difference.

In my 20 years working in industry I've never been

accused once of breaking the confidence of an employee. That's pretty remarkable when you think about it. You have to sell the program, and that takes time, but I would imagine it takes time off-site as well as on-site. Mostly what we need is programs, and *where* they exist, I think, is not as important as *having them*. Having them takes some selling.

Audience:

What is the attitude in industry toward workers who are unwilling to look at their problems? Even though people around them are aware that a problem exists, some workers themselves are unwilling to seek help.

Mr. Van Jones:

I see a change in attitudes. The stigma of alcohol or drug abuse has somewhat diminished over the years. That's probably the chief reason why people volunteer for treatment at early stages. There has been a change in attitudes of workers because of awareness programs, because of media announcements and, in general, the diminished stigma of having a problem with alcoholism or drugs. I still think there's a great stigma attached to mental illness. The mentally troubled employee is somewhat more reluctant to seek out help. As the doctor stated, he's often ridiculed upon returning to the work force, because he was in the proverbial "nut house." But in alcohol and drug abuse, people do come forward for help at early stages.

Ms. Nelson:

I think we all share this realization that the stigma is reduced. One of the things that occurs among women who are organized is that they will see that somebody in that group has a problem. In New York City, we have a considerable alcoholism and drug abuse program for women. The program reaches out in all kinds of ways to touch base with women. There's a lot of attention given to it and the women are spotting each other and pushing each other in.

Audience:

We talk about the employee who won't look at his problems, but what about those in management who won't look at the conditions that cause problems?

Ms. Nelson:

I would like us to confront the fact that changes need to be made in situations that are causing people terrible anguish. While a person can be helped by counseling or hospitalization, he can also be helped by changing the situation so that he will be relieved of this abrasion.

There's sexual harassment at work. There are the family roles of who does most work, which has been pretty well researched at this point. A working woman does 4.1 hours of work at home a day, and the husband of the working woman does 1.4; the husband of a non-working woman also does 1.4. So, we've got sexual distribution there which could be changed to alleviate abrasion.

There is a lot that can be done about automation, and of course assembly lines. In offices, we're installing a lot of equipment that shouldn't be installed without the co-operative advice, consent, and feedback from the workers who are going to be using the equipment. And there should be quite a lot of care given to *how* that machinery is used, the time spans it is used, and when workers should take a break and not be permitted to watch that screen any longer. There are numerous situations that could be changed to save people a great deal of stress and anguish.

Audience:

It has occurred to me in listening to all of your comments that there has been a great effort on the part of many of the larger organizations, corporations and government agencies, to address the issue that we've been talking about today. But it seems to me that there is a significant segment of the work force that does not have access to the kinds of programs we're talking about. The larger corporations have resources that many smaller companies don't have. What kinds of alternatives could there be for smaller companies?

Dr. Gallagher:

What you're basically talking about is the need for occupational medical clinics. An industrial park of comparably small firms totalling thousands of employees should have an occupational medical clinic. To have one, employers have to provide resources and band together. There are very few people who can afford up-front investment in a medical building and the equipment needed. But together—and maybe employees should contribute, too—they could afford it.

This has been tried on an experimental basis in a few areas. But, for the most part, they didn't last more than two or three years because the financial base was not there. In other words, they had the facility built and equipped but the companies did not provide a guaranteed source of income. Any facility like that will need five years to become established. That has been pretty much the experience of most free-standing occupational medical clinics. Until industry decides that this is the cost-effective way to go, employees of small businesses must get health care at the local hospital emergency room. That is very, very expensive.

Ms. Nelson:

The Amalgamated Clothing Workers and the International Ladies Garment Workers have clinics and child care centers which they share with the community where they're located.

Audience:

Many of the employee assistance programs that you're talking about are addressing issues to specific populations, such as the alcoholic and the substance abuser. What about other groups, specifically those individuals who are losing their jobs, or those who have already lost their jobs? What types of assistances are being made available for these individuals?

Dr. Hess:

Less and less, I would assume, considering the present Federal administration. Less and less money is being given for such projects.

Dr. Mashikian:

Just before an employee loses his job the company should be sensitive to the mental health needs of that employee, and anticipate those needs. It becomes an even greater responsibility of that company if the employee who is about to lose his job is already known to them as having had a problem. When it comes to the jitters in terms of those who are afraid that their jobs might be eliminated, I still believe that education plays the major role. We can do a lot more if we trained our top managers in lines of human behavior.

Ms. Nelson:

I think that this response on job jitters is a good one. There's a lot that can be done internally in the organization. But when you're talking about job loss, it's different. If you speak to the people who've lost their jobs because their plant closed, you hear their guilt, they think they're responsible because that plant closed. There's enormous loneliness, just extreme loneliness and there's a lot of doubling up of families for money reasons.

What I'm thinking about is organizing of the unemployed. This is a historic practice; we engaged in it during the Depression. Unemployed people have got to have somebody beside them. They're floating around. A guy goes off in the morning and tells his wife he's going to go look for a job. But he doesn't know what to do with himself, he doesn't know where to go.

If he's a laid-off Ford employee, he hears, "Oh, you're that Ford guy who closed the plant down because of your low productivity. I wouldn't hire you." And the loneliness is just desperate. I think if there were a way to simply get the unemployed together and moving towards something—it doesn't give them their money, I understand that—it would give them back their confidence and their sense of the real world.

Chapter 3

THE INDUSTRIAL WORKER: OVEREXPOSED AND UNDEREMPLOYED— A TALE OF TWO EVILS

Kenneth B. Miller, M.D.

During the past six years in which I've been involved in occupational and environmental medicine, I have been exposed, if you will, to countless interactions with industrial workers, service workers, who have frequently voiced to me their concerns, their distress, and even what might have been seen as their symptoms regarding the problems in

Dr. Miller is, at present, the Occupational Health Physician for the Oil, Chemical and Atomic Workers International Union in Washington, D.C. Prior to this, he was Medical Director of the Workers' Institute for Safety and Health, a labor-sponsored research and education consulting group involved in issues concerning workplace safety and health. As well, he presently holds appointments as Assistant Professor of Community Health at the Albert Einstein College of Medicine and as a Lecturer in the Environmental Sciences Laboratory of the Mt. Sinai School of Medicine, both in New York City. His previous background includes an undergraduate degree in Psychology at Brooklyn College and training in internal medicine. He is a Board-Certified Specialist in Preventive Medicine/Occupational Medicine.

living and coping with very difficult circumstances at work, during extraordinarily difficult times.

And today, more than ever before, the blue-collar and pink-collar work forces are unemployed, underemployed, and often overexposed to a vast array of neuro-behavioral toxins and environmental stressors, both in their work and community environments. And we see this happening all over the country at this time. It's with regard to these factors and their effects on the mental health of workers and their families that I will discuss some of what we know about these problems, and much about what we don't know of these etiologies and their effects, and how we may increase our understanding of what types of intervention may be useful in ameliorating these conditions which may induce these psycho-social disorders.

It's clear to me that such a discussion of the mental health impact of unemployment, as well as workplace toxicity, is an extraordinarily broad topic. Therefore, in the interest of a deeper and more focused analysis of certain specific problems, I will make some notable and rather important omissions of such factors as the predisposition to mental illness, individual variabilities, and the role of other non-occupational etiologies in the causation of mental health problems. For the most part, I will focus on the role of the workplace—stress, sexual harassment, productivity pressures, etc. As well, most of my remarks will be confined and limited largely to industrial and service workers, thereby excluding most executive and managerial employees.

Perhaps some background would be of use for those of you who are not familiar with occupational medicine in its present-day form. It's my belief that we are in the midst of a very occult and somewhat silent epidemic of occupational disease. I believe now that what was once the tip of an iceberg in terms of work-related problems is now emerging, and we're well beyond the tip, as far as I can see. The Bureau of Labor Statistics of the Department of Labor revealed that there are approximately 400,000 cases of occupational disease every year in the country, and 100,000 work-related deaths each year. (That's twice the number of deaths in the Vietnam war during the entire time we were involved there.) That equals out to about one death every six minutes of working time.

As we've also seen, there are serious problems spilling over into our communities—I don't have to say anything more than Times Beach, or Love Canal, or Three Mile Island for all of you to understand what I'm talking about. The mental uncertainty of living with those kinds of exposures down the road is, we believe, clearly related to certain kinds of mental health problems.

Much of the disease that we're seeing today, of course, is the result of seeds sown in the past of exposures that have occurred 20, 30, 40 years ago, and it is a diabolical twist of fate, in some sense, that a slight exposure to a carcinogen 20 years ago or 30 years ago can later on produce a malignancy or other chronic disease.

However, we are today sowing new seeds as well, and exposures are continuing in our factories, and in our hospitals, and in our service employment situations. This guarantees that I will unfortunately be working into the year 2000 and beyond, because of the latent period that is evident with these problems.

In terms of cancer, which is a feared word for many people, and causes much distress, the following facts must be noted. In 1978, three agencies, the National Cancer Institute, the National Institute for Occupational Safety and Health, and the National Institute of Environmental Health Sciences, published a widely-reported document in which they estimated, on the basis of exposure to industrial workers of nine or ten different carcinogens, including asbestos, benzine, arsenic, and a few others, that somewhere between 20 and 38 percent of all cancers in this country are related to occupational exposures. That's a fairly significant figure, and while the study has been a source of some controversy, and other estimates have been put forward, in my experience the number is somewhat accurate.

Right now, today, there are 1.2 million workers who are daily exposed to benzine at levels that we believe are dangerous. There are a million people still exposed to arsenic, and it's one of the oldest known carcinogens. So I do think that against this backdrop of occupational disease, physical disease, and mental disease, we have a whole host of problems that people need to be concerned about.

Much to the surprise of most employees and employers, physicians, and other health professionals, the history of this problem and the relationship between workplace exposure and mental illness dates back to some of medicine's earliest recognition of diseases. The oft-quoted description, "mad as a hatter" in Lewis Carroll's story of "Alice in Wonderland," is derived from the bizarre behavior of workers in the felting process who were exposed to mercury in the course of their employment in the hatting industry. Thus the term, "mad as a hatter." This dates back a very long time. Mercury does accumulate in the central nervous system and can induce severe neurologic and psychologic pathology.

Recent reports have documented the ubiquitous exposure to lead throughout the whole history of the Roman Empire. In fact, a recent study attributes much of the irrational behavior of Nero fiddling as Rome burned and the irrational behavior of other elites of Roman society to lead exposure. In fact, there was an article in *The New York Times* recently actually trying to attribute the fall of the Roman Empire in some measure to this widespread exposure to lead through lead pottery and lead crucibles used for cooking and eating. A very interesting theory.

Lead poisoning is still a common problem in industry today and we are still struggling with getting a more effective lead standard put in place and having it enforced by the Occupational Safety and Health Administration. These are daily ongoing problems. In 1713, Bernadino Ramazinni, the father of occupational medicine—for those of you who are interested in father figures—in his seminal treatise, "De Morbis Artificum" which in Latin means, "The Diseases of Workers," gives the earliest known description of central and peripheral nervous system effects of lead poisoning. He observed that potters "become palsied, then they become paralytic, splenetic, lethargic, cachectic, and toothless so that one rarely sees a potter whose face is not cadaverous."

The problems today, though not as profound and the exposures not nearly as severe, still persist nonetheless. Today we often characterize the worker with lead-induced encephalopathy as irritable, which I guess is a substitute for splenetic, lethargic, and depressed. His sleep patterns are often disturbed, and certain endocrine functions may be impaired. These symptoms, particularly the irritability, are often the earliest clinical indicators of exposure and are common presenting complaints. And we still have thousands of people—smelters, and workers making the batteries for all our cars and trucks and vehicles, potters in industry, and even potters in their homes, artists—who are still overexposed to lead.

Thus, the problem has not sprung upon us *de novo*, as Ramazinni described illnesses in some 25 occupations in 1713 including the diseases of learned men and the diseases of Jews and corpse bearers. While it is not a new problem, and it is not solely related to recent industrial development as we have often heard, needless to say the Industrial Revolution and the rapid emergence of the petro-chemical era has both broadened the scope and the magnitude of the problem and somewhat intensified the aftermath of the diseases left in their wake.

This extraordinary industrial growth in the last 50 years or so, and our increasing dependence on synthetic materials based on and derived from petroleum, has lead us to a situation where we now find that we have approximately 60,000 chemicals in the stream of commerce with about 600 to 1,000 new substances being introduced yearly. Many of these substances are not or have not been adequately tested for their physiologic toxicities in animals or in humans. It's obvious to say that it is a more difficult task to appropriately screen substances using animal models for their behavioral effects. Indeed, even indepth epidemiologic approaches to these underlying neurologic and neurobehavioral problems due to exposure have been sporadic, at best, and the literature is severely lacking.

Additionally, in my view, our efforts to regulate industrial exposures, have been insufficient for those materials whose toxicity is well known, for example, lead. Also, appropriate documentation is scarce. We still have only standards of limits of exposure for 300 to 400 of the substances; that represents a very small proportion of the 50,000 to 60,000 chemicals that I mentioned earlier. The literature is replete, however, with case reports and series of cases of severe neuro-behavioral derangement due to workplace exposure. And these neuro-toxicities fall in a wide range of categories; we have many substances that cause peripheral neuropathy, we have many substances that cause an organic-brain-syndrome-like effect, interfering with cognitive functions, and then we have substances which actually induce emotional disorders. And I'm going to briefly run through a few of the more common or dramatic ones.

One of the most interesting and oldest reports comes about from the rubber vulcanizations and viscous rayon industries. Back in 1856, in the vulcanization of rubber process, it was reported that a chemical known as carbon disulphide induced severe acute psychosis with delusions and hallucinations in workers exposed. Employees actually leaped from factory windows committing suicide during this process of overexposure necessitating the installation of bars on the windows as a preventive measure. This was certainly not the most appropriate preventive health measure, but at least it stopped them from jumping out.

Between the 1900's and the 1950's, among the most significant neuro-toxic chemicals that came into wide use were carbon tetrachloride, methylene chloride, trichloroethylene, toluene and numerous other widely-used industrial solvents. These are used today and in the past in such processes as dry-cleaning and de-greasing, and any machine or factory operation in which materials are contaminated with oil and grease uses one or another of these solvents for the degreasing process. These are known to produce memory loss, vertigo, personality changes, ataxia, peripheral neuropathy, tremors, stupor, and they do remain in wide use in many industrial applications, and exposures both dermal and via inhalation are still occurring.

Often, however, the clinical picture of direct central nervous system toxicity appears to mimic the picture of organic brain syndrome or pre-senile dementia, as can be seen with chronic exposure to carbon monoxide, as in fire fighters, or garage attendants, or toll and tunnel employees. This can induce central nervous system damage.

In other situations, the effects resemble a profound interruption of cognitive faculties, as was the case with the widespread exposure to a chemical known as polybromi-nated-biphenals, or PBB, which is a chemical that was found in more than 90 percent of the population of the state of Michigan when this fire retardant chemical was accidently and mistakenly added to cattle and chicken feed and bio-accumulated in the food chain. It was the Michigan farmers who consumed their own dairy and meat products who showed the most severe symptoms because they had the highest exposures. They experienced profound leth-argy—sleeping 18 to 20 hours a day—and severe cognitive dysfunction manifested by inability to perform simple and usual tasks. We had reports of people getting on a tractor and not being able to figure out how to operate it, after they had worked on it for 20 years.

The term psycho-vegetative syndrome was applied to these people and it's been used in other halogenated hy-drocarbon poisoning episodes. The long-term conse-quences remain unknown. Similarly I'm sure many of you have heard about the Kepone situation in Hopewell, Vir-ginia where a pesticide which was manufactured in a plant was released into the environment; you still can't fish in the James River and that was more than 10 years ago.

This poisoning of the workers left a large percentage of the workers impotent, irreversibly sterile, and with marked personality changes. These people unfortunately are often left to suffer in silence because they are far be-yond the reach of the mental health community.

So there have been some fairly serious disasters. How-ever, more commonly, the disorders are much more subtle, more slowly progressive and chronic in nature, and have no immediately attributable etiology which is separable from other causes. Yet, I would like to make the case to you that the recognition of this relationship between ex-posure and illness is crucial for a number of reasons.

First and foremost, in terms of research information,

recognition has proceeded somewhat from studies done by the National Institute of Occupational Safety and Health, in which they have recognized a number of chemicals as being neuro-toxic and have set standards based on their neuro-toxicity. Some 22 of the 32 chemicals that they have set standards for that are neuro-toxic are standards that were set to limit the neuro-toxic effects. There is further work going on with a battery of psychometric testing, which has been developed in Finland where they're doing a lot of work on the mental health effects of low-level exposure to solvents and other chemicals. So there is some research going on, but I'm here to talk to you about what you can do as practitioners and clinicians in the field to help you to recognize some of these problems.

Perhaps I can best illustrate how this is done and why this is important by a case that I was recently involved in. I was asked about a man who had worked in an aluminum refinery in Oregon. Over a period of a few months, this man's wife began to notice that he was becoming increasingly irritable, depressed, had developed a slight tremor, and as the man had no previous history of mental disorder, his profound personality changes, including wife-beating and some child abuse, were quite noticeable and quite alarming.

The situation progressed in severity, and after a period of psychiatric consultation, some medication, and a period of hospitalization, he was released, apparently without any indication of what was to come. He returned home and put a .38-calibre pistol in his mouth and killed himself. It was only after this event that it was recognized by an astute union officer who called me that manganese—a metal that is extensively used in metal refining, and in fact, deposits in the central nervous system and can lead to a somewhat similar clinical picture—was in use in this man's work area.

Unfortunately, nowhere in the chart was an occupational history taken of the case, nor was manganesism, a known disease, considered in the differential diagnosis of the man's problem. Thus, there is no information now— which could have been gotten when he was alive had this been considered—of serum or tissue level of the manganese in his body, which would have helped establish the diagnosis. And now the family is struggling, in addition to the numerous mental health problems that arise from the case, with whether or not to exhume the body, because they want manganese levels so that they can perhaps take the case to Workers' Compensation. I will say more about Workers' Compensation with regard to mental health problems in a few moments.

I think these examples are instructive in that they illustrate at least two or three major problems we face in establishing a work-related etiology for mental problems. First and foremost is the fact that most workers in the United States today still do not have the right, nor the opportunity, to know what they are working with, and what the possible health risks are as the result of exposure. A few states, such as New York, for example, have recently passed state-wide laws called "Right to Know" laws which empower workers to request or demand of their employer what they're exposed to and the toxic health effects. Most jurisdictions still retain the employers' prerogative of not revealing the identity of the substances nor the health effects that may result. Thus, in this case, little could be done by the employee himself to alert his physician to look for these problems and to be aware of the consequences. As well, it would have been important to look at other workers in the area who might have been prevented from developing a similar outcome.

Secondly, of course, as I mentioned earlier, none of the physicians involved had enough training in medical school. Most medical schools do not train people very well, or at all in many cases, in the art or science, if you will, of occupational medicine, in particular occupational history-taking. So the physicians, or the other mental health workers in the case, were not able to identify the problem.

And thirdly, and a major stumbling block in establishing an etiology, is the multi-factorial nature of mental illness and the complexities of accurate diagnosis and attributing causality to specific factors. This is, as I said before, a major problem, and it is often difficult to identify the culprit here.

Thus far, though, I've just touched upon a direct relationship between industrial exposures and mental health. There is however, as I've alluded to earlier, an equally important set of related problems which are surfacing which deal with the indirect effects of work-related illnesses of any kind, be they mental health, or neuro-toxic problems, or not, on the families of industrial workers which I would briefly like to mention.

These problems arise, I believe, from three important principles:

One, that illness of any kind, work-related or not, can induce severe economic and emotional dislocation on those affected and their families.

Two, that industrial workers—fathers and mothers, husbands and wives, alike—can often act as vectors, if you will, for exposure by carrying toxic materials on their clothing into the home and unwittingly exposing other family members. And this is a real problem.

When I was trained at Mt. Sinai, where a lot of the original work on asbestos was done, we knew of numerous cases of 25- and 30-year-old young men and women who were dying of mesothelioma, a cancer that is known to be related only to asbestos exposure. We were hard-pressed at first to figure out where this exposure came from until we found out that a family member was an asbestos worker and every day the son or daughter would come home and give him a hug as they came home from work. From that asbestos exposure, 30 years later, they had a rapidly malignant, highly progressive tumor; the mean survival for mesothelioma is less than six months.

In fact, in the studies of the families of asbestos workers done at Mt. Sinai, we found that approximately 60 percent, almost two-thirds of the wives of asbestos workers, had visible X-ray changes compatible with asbestos exposure on their chest X-rays. Perhaps some of you recently saw a "Nova" program that dealt with this asbestos. It was quite heartbreaking to see the father and mother of a child who had died of mesothelioma at age 12.

The third problem that we face is that we're beginning to see negative reproductive outcome in families, such as miscarriages, stillbirths, birth defects, impotence and sterility, and these can and do result from on-the-job exposures. I've mentioned Kepone, we've seen this with vinyl chloride as well, where miscarriage rates among the spouses of workers exposed to vinyl chloride have increased rates of miscarriages and a number of other things. Recently, in Schenectady, New York, three or four years ago, there was a pesticide that was being manufactured called Orzalin that was supposedly implicated in inducing cardiovascular birth defects in children.

Our methods for measuring the burden that is placed on the finely-woven fabric of a family's mental health by a child who will have to live in an institution as the result of a severe birth defect, or by the death of a spouse whose terminal cancer is the result of washing the asbestos-contaminated clothing of her husband, are not well-developed. The guilt and anguish that normally coincide with illness are frequently exacerbated in these situations by a feeling of betrayal and anger. In my experience, an employee who is made aware of the cause of the disease feels that the company or the government or someone should have told him, should have warned him, should have been protecting him; he often feels that the standards should be protecting him, which they often, unfortunately, do not, particularly against chronic disease. There is that feeling commonly when I deal with patients who have been exposed to asbestos, as it has been known since 1935 that this was a harmful substance. Knowingly-concealed information generates a significant amount of frustration and anger among people who have been harmed. There is, in turn, greater frustration on the part of these people who have nowhere to turn because there is nothing we can do to treat these illnesses. They are only preventable.

The consequences in terms of the mental health of such people, and there are many in the situation, remain virtually unexplored. Few of us can truly understand this frustration, this pain, that develops from the cruel twist of fate of latent cancers. As I said, this can only be heightened by the lack of access to redress from the frequently unavailable and responsible parties. Yet, frequently in my personal experience I do encounter these situations and they are very, very difficult.

Now, what of compensation? I mentioned the role of Workers' Compensation and the importance of recognizing these work-related problems.

First of all, in a 1980 study by the Department of Labor it was noted that for people who were severely disabled from occupational diseases, only five percent of the victims received Workers' Compensation. Five percent. Twenty percent of the people received no benefits at all from any source. The remaining 75 percent we find on Social Security disability, on veterans benefits, getting their health care through other mechanisms. It ought to be remembered that Workers' Compensation only pays for medical costs and loss of work time. It does not pay for grief and

suffering or pain, or any of those other attributes that accompany these problems. There is often a long delay.
Studies show that the average waiting time for the settle-
ment of a Workers' Compensation case is often more than
a year. For this reason, many people settle out of court or
don't bother to go through the process, because the delay
is often so long.

Many people are not aware of the fact that Workers'
Compensation takes away the right of the worker to directly
sue his or her employer. It is a no-fault insurance system
designed to block that kind of litigation.

So, we do have some problems with Workers' Compensation in terms of the system. The number of mental
health cases that enter the system are severely limited to
those occupations like air traffic controllers and others
where stress and other workplace factors are well-documented and well-known.

Finally, if we do not have good clinical recognition by
mental health professionals as to the relationship between
workplace exposure and disease because these kinds of
questions are not being asked, the chances to win a Workers' Compensation case are very, very small. Oftentimes,
in many of the cases I've participated in, it becomes a battle
of the network experts. There are doctors and specialists
from all kinds of different universities, or organizations,
who offer conflicting opinions which frequently result in
inadequate resolution of the problem.

I want to switch from the problem that we face with
occupational diseases to a more acute problem that we're
facing now. This is the problem of the health outcomes of
unemployment in industrial workers. Much has been written about this in the lay media. I do want to call your attention to a study that was recently released by Dr. M.
Harvey Brenner, a professor of health services administration at Johns Hopkins, who went back and looked at

records between the period 1940 to 1973. He was asked by Congress to generate a projection as to what the consequences would be of a one percent increase in unemployment. And he found that a one percent increase in the unemployment rate corresponded to a 4.1 percent increase in suicides, a 5.7 increase in homicides, a 4.3 increase for males and a 2.3 percentage increase for females in the rate of admissions to psychiatric hospitals, and a 1.9 percent increase in deaths from heart disease, cirrhosis, and other chronic stress-related diseases.

Another study found that unemployed breadwinners frequently suffered from high blood pressure, insomnia, nervous exhaustion, and anxiety; and these symptoms and these problems, of course, spilled directly over into other family members. Wife-beating and child abuse are rising dramatically in areas of high unemployment, and alcoholism as well is reportedly increasing. At the same time, job loss is also followed by a loss of health insurance and medical care coverage, particularly for people who are long-term unemployed, as you all know. And this I believe is a particularly cruel irony because at this point, unemployment is precipitating many of the diseases that require intervention, and the access to medical care for those who need it is severely limited by the fact that people don't have any health insurance.

Today, in fact, there are more than 25 million people who have no health care coverage at all. That's a little more than one in 10.

The feeling and anxiety that accompany job loss are obvious, as are the increase in suicides, health problems and prison incarcerations in times of serious economic disruptions. Less clear, however, are the subtle effects of long periods of joblessness, which are often accompanied by severe loss of self-esteem, a lack of identity, and feelings of inadequacy as the primary role of primary breadwinner in the family evaporates. These problems can probably be explored by future research efforts, because I fear that the changes wrought by this period of economic dislocation may be long-lasting, and leave behind an unconscious residue of self-doubt and insecurity. People are really shaken by these events, and Dr. Brenner's research has given us an indication in that regard, in that he notes that the effects of unemployment on the indicator-rates—that is suicides, admissions to psychiatric facilities, etc.—may persist for as long as six years after the increase in the joblessness rate. And for the laid-off worker with 25 years of employment— and sometimes 25 years of exposure to a carcinogen—the combination of acute or prolonged unemployment and the loss of health insurance, and a cancer latency that is ticking away, may truly be a formidable definition of adding insult to injury.

Only the terminally cynical would suggest—as some have to me—that unemployment is the appropriate cure for a hazardous job.

In closing, I do not want to leave you with the feeling that all is doom and gloom with the industrial worker, although I'd be less than honest if I said that these were not extraordinarily trying times for these people. While many of the problems I have raised are systemic in our society, and therefore require broad preventive strategies for change, there is much that can be done by individuals who practice in the mental health arena.

I would encourage all of you to become more aware of these issues and factors, and to be sensitive to them in your patients. We must all maintain a high index of suspicion about the role of workplace exposures and the etiology of mental illness, and inquire in detail about these factors. Moreover, I'm sure that it would be bad form for me to close a presentation at a conference like this if I did not send out the call for further research in the area. And so, in an effort to appease my ancestors in the medical profession, let me sincerely appeal to those of you who happen to be involved in mental health research to consider and explore these factors in your research, and the potential interactions with other etiologic factors.

There are vast black holes in our understanding and these gaps desperately need to be filled. Further, there is an enormous need for collaborative research efforts among public health researchers, epidemiologists, occupational health specialists, and mental health professionals to further clarify and tease apart these complex interactive phenomena. But let us be sure that further study is not used as a substitute for concerted action toward preventing these work-related problems. It's clear that the disease of overexposure and underemployment are largely preventable. What it will take to prevent them is a societal commitment to clean, safe workplaces, and a full employment economy with job security and the administrative policies to make them a reality.

I think that we all have a lot of work to do in this area.

SELECTED READING

Johnson, B.L. and Anger, W.K. "Behavioral Toxicology" in *Environmental and Occupational Medicine*, W. Rom, ed., 1982.

Last, J.M. ed. *Public Health and Preventive Medicine*, 11th ed. Appleton/Century/Crofts, New York, 1980.

Proctor, W.H. and Hughes, J.P. *Chemical Hazards of the Workplace*, J.B. Lippincott, Co., Philadelphia, 1978.

Spencer, P.S. and Schaumberg, H.H. *Experimental and Clinical Neurotoxicology*, Williams and Wilkins, London, 1980.

DISCUSSION

Chaired by speaker Dr. Miller, this panel included: Walter J. Donheiser, Ph.D., Associate Director of Psychological Services, South Oaks Hospital; Charles Winick, Ph.D., Technical Consultant, Central Labor Rehabilitation Council of New York, Inc.; and Richard M. Zoppa, M.D., Senior Psychiatrist, South Oaks Hospital.

Dr. Miller:

I believe there is a need for an interaction between the occupational health community and the mental health community. There are a lot of physical hazards and chemical exposures that cause disease, and regardless of what the cause of the disease is, they induce a significant amount of anxiety and concern. In addition, there are special problems related to occupational medicine, of workers feeling "at risk." For example, if you know you've been exposed to a carcinogen, you have to live with that for 20, 30 years, waiting for this time to tick away, and asking, "Am I going to be the one?" These are the kinds of questions and concerns I get in the clinical end of my practice.

Dr. Donheiser:

I'd like to discuss the question of under-utilization in the workplace. It means not only unemployed. I take it to also mean that workers frequently find themselves in the position where their talents are not being utilized, and they end up with a feeling of futility. This also ties in with self-actualization: a person feels like he is destined to perform tasks below his capacity, and that he is not using his talents and ability to their full potential. With that comes a feeling of frustration, or depression. This is true of professionals, of factory workers, of everybody. This frequently leads to a burnout, to just mechanically going through a routine.

Dr. Zoppa:

As we are addressing how important it is for workers to be properly cared for, it strikes me that this century has seen more progress in caring for all sorts of workers than any other century in history. So, although we're far from where we should be, I think we probably have made some giant steps. For example, I'd hate to have been working in the Welsh coal mines in the early part of the 19th century. Obviously, the Industrial Revolution and modern technology have brought a lot of stresses to the so-called modernized world. We don't see as much asbestosis or pneumoconiosis. We see instead people who have problems with other chemicals, mainly alcohol. These chemical problems are quite serious and reflect the stresses of today.

Dr. Miller:

There's a recent move among employers to conduct alcohol and drug screening programs; testing urine for marijuana abuse, supervisors noting a worker's behavior, smelling alcohol on his breath. This creates a lot of concern, anxiety, and anger on the part of the industrial workers who feel it's an infringement on their personal life.

Do you run into this problem?

Dr. Zoppa:

We deal with various large and small companies, and these companies usually have employees who have been trained to pick up, for example, alcoholism. Many of them are recovered alcoholics who have worked for years with the company and now have this function. Yes, there is always a certain amount of resistance on the part of the individual but usually it can be dealt with very effectively if it's done with tact. Usually by the time a worker's drinking is noticed by anybody, the worker will either have accumulated absences, or is coming in to work but not being very effective.

And when a supervisor approaches that worker and says, "You know, you're really not doing your job," at that point it's very hard for him to deny that there is a problem.

Audience:

What about the employee who is suspected of being a cocaine user? I had that situation in my company. The supervisor threatened the person and told him to take a blood test; if the worker didn't take this test, the supervisor said the worker would lose his job. The person did take the test which found some substance. He was fired just the same.

That's infringement of employee rights.

Dr. Donheiser:

From the hospital's point of view, what we see is the use of job jeopardy as leverage to get the person in treatment. Many people who come here for alcohol or drug treatment have been placed on job jeopardy and told if they do not receive treatment, they will be fired.

Dr. Winick:

I formerly directed the Musicians' Clinic, a New York City treatment program for addicted musicians, and also have done large-scale studies of addicted nurses and physicians. On the basis of these studies, it proved possible to develop a theory of role deprivation and role strain as precursors of problems with workers who will have difficulties with substances like alcohol and drugs.

In terms of the labor movement's attitude toward alcohol and drug matters, there is a clear policy on these matters developed by the AFL-CIO Community Services Department. The policy states that job performance is the only consideration that would permit management to discuss or question a worker's drug use. That is, what the individual does in his or her private life, is his or her own business. If, however, there is a deteriorating job performance, if there are accidents, if people don't show up regularly for work, if they regularly come back from lunch a half-hour late with slurred speech, that's a different story. There are a series of recommended steps delineated to identify the impaired worker who is a drinker or a drug user. Labor feels that under such circumstances, it's perfectly proper—and in fact desirable—for labor and management to cooperate in calling the impaired performance to the worker's attention and saying that this is not tolerable and he must take action or lose his job.

Now let me just make a few brief comments on underemployment and overexposure. They are very closely linked. In fact, from the labor point of view, they are essentially the same problem. Why is that? First of all, with high unemployment, people don't have much latitude in getting jobs, therefore, a person may be forced to take a job at which he or she is underemployed. Secondly, many employees who are unhappy because they are underemployed, sense the job market is weak, and are afraid to leave their jobs because they feel they will get nothing else. They'd rather have something—however unpleasant and unsatisfactory—than have nothing.

I did a study a number of years ago, and developed a scale of atony to measure listlessness, lack of appetite, lack of involvement with reality, lack of responsiveness. I was able to study two large work organizations, one, a building service company, and the other, a New York City newspaper. I took the one-third of the populations that had the highest atony scores—that is, they were the least "with it"—and I interviewed them. I was interested in seeing what factors were correlated with their lack of responsiveness to reality. The largest single factor was underemployment. They were not functioning at a level at which they felt capable of functioning. It wasn't pay, it wasn't their titles, and it was not the work conditions. They knew that they were unhappy and uncomfortable, they weren't too keen on coming to work, but until these interviews many hadn't been able to verbalize the reasons for their unhappiness.

I'd like to discuss three particular kinds of workers who come to us at Central Labor Rehabilitation Council for help with problems.

We see a disproportionately high number of people who are television industry technicians working in studios, at tape machines and the like. They are high school graduates who average as much as $70,000 a year. The reason for the high income is overtime: they work around the clock, they work weekends, they have to be ready whenever they're called. Yet, these people with very large incomes come looking for help for a variety of problems. Why are they coming in for help? Well, one reason is they work with famous stars and superstars and yet they are anonymous. Also, they have to work under enormous pressure—if one of these machines break down when something is on the air, there's trouble. Because they work at night, and they sometimes work all weekend for 48 hours at a stretch, there's great pressure to ease the tension by, say, taking cocaine or relaxing in other ways that might lead to difficulty. They work such long hours they never learn to spend their money intelligently. They come in with problems that sound relatively vague: they don't really know why they need help but they know something isn't right.

Two other unions among those which send members to us for help are those representing exterminators and bridge painters.

When the exterminators, who work with unpleasant chemicals, come into a stranger's home, nobody really wants to see them. They're symbols of whatever it is they're supposed to be getting rid of. There are all sorts of jokes about them.

A bridge painter may spend much of his work life working on just one bridge. It takes about six or eight months to paint a bridge. By the time painters finish one end, they have to go back to the other end and start all over again. By the very nature of the work, it never ends. And there they are on the same bridge; it's almost a permanent reminder that what they're doing is not satisfactory.

I mention these three kinds of workers because they're all relatively well paid and have good work benefits, but they're disproportionately likely to seek help for a variety of personal problems. In each case a slightly different aspect of their social environment is involved, but it has to do with Dr. Miller's point of underemployment and overexposure.

Dr. Miller:

I would like to respond with two personal experiences.

At Albert Einstein College of Medicine, I ran a screening project with exterminators to measure the effects of exposure to pesticides on their blood. In that process I spent a work day with an exterminator. And I found that what you're saying is absolutely true. I went with a particular exterminator to office after office in Manhattan from 8:00 a.m. to 3:00 p.m. The poor fellow. In addition to the exposure to the pesticides and having to worry about washing his hands, and mixing the stuff and spilling it, as soon as he walked in, everybody said, "Oh, here comes the bug man. Yuck." It was the most abusive sort of thing I've ever experienced. People would leave the office to avoid this poor fellow. It was just really terrible.

What I find interesting—and everybody sees it from their own perspective—is that you mentioned both bridge painters and exterminators and a number of reasons why they may have mental health problems. Well, the bells in my head automatically go off because I know that what both painters and exterminators have in common is that they both work with central nervous system toxins. With painters, it's solvents in paint, which are toxic to the central nervous system.

If a bridge painter is working 200 feet up on the George Washington Bridge and if he starts to get woozy from the solvents and the paint thinner, he *has* to be worried, and the fear is ever-present. He also worries about chronic central nervous system toxicity that occurs with long-term solvent exposure. Exterminators must also deal with knowing that they are working with carcinogens and other toxic chemicals which are making them sick.

In fact, the exterminator who I worked with for a day gave me a classic history of symptoms related to exposure at the end of his workday, after he'd been mixing and spraying, and getting the chemicals on his hands. Remember, chemicals are absorbed through the skin. After a full day's work, he was nauseated; I was nauseated after just two or three hours of breathing the fumes.

There are both physiological and psychological interactions in the work world that are causing mental ill health.

Dr. Zoppa:
The variable is the individual. If you take 10 individuals and subject them to the same stress, one will have a psychotic episode, another may become depressed, another may turn to alcohol, and seven others will yell at their spouses as a way of dealing with stress.

Dr. Miller:

If we fill this room with asbestos today, so thick you couldn't see, statistically 45 percent of the people in this room would develop cancer. The real question is why the other 55 percent don't. The same thing is true with lead. There is a spectrum of illness with lead poisoning.

A man is brought into the emergency room and his wife's complaint is, "He's just so irritable now, he's horrible to live with." You take his work history and you find out he's got low-level chronic lead exposure. He hadn't developed abdominal colic or other physiological symptoms. He had mental aberrations that were picked up first. And he may be working right next to a person who is fine. There is the opposite example of five people who were tearing down an elevated highway, and they were burning through layers and layers of lead-based paint to get to the steel. All five came to the Mt. Sinai Hospital emergency room with lead poisoning. Some were irritable, some had a little belly pain, some were having neurologic symptoms. We had one guy who was absolutely fine, but he was scared because everyone else was going, so he went along for the ride. There is the spectrum of illness with neuro-behavior, and that's what makes it very difficult to diagnose, as well as to counsel.

I see people who come to me who have been exposed to asbestos for 10 years, and they read in the newspaper that it causes cancer. They are scared to death. They come to me and ask what can you do for me? How can you help me? There's really nothing I can offer them. I can tell them the statistical chances of developing cancer. I can tell them not to worry because not everyone gets it, and you may not be the one who does. I try to assure them, make them more comfortable, and yet knowing the statistics, I'm in conflict about not telling them the truth. First, exposure creates neuro-toxicological problems, and, second, the knowledge of exposure creates a mental health burden, or a fear or anxiety reaction. I see it so frequently, especially in the industrial setting.

Audience:

As mental health workers, we try to prevent mental illness. We encourage people to go for psychiatric attention. But is it still asked on personnel application blanks, "Have you ever gone for psychiatric help?"

Dr. Zoppa:

I tell my patients to be discriminative—whatever they're applying for—a driver's license or a job. I tell them to let their consciences be the guide. It's up to them as to whether or not they want it known. I realize that there is a certain amount of stigma. We'd like to think there isn't, but there is.

I know of a company which encourages its employees to come in and get help—then after they get help, they are fired. Word got around very quickly and many employees weren't seeking help, obviously, because they didn't want to lose their jobs. Unfortunately the information cannot always be withheld because of third-party payment.

Audience:

How does a person find out if there's something toxic in the workplace? Can you call in someone to test the work environment?

Dr. Miller:

That's an excellent question, and requires a rather lengthy answer if I were to list all the resources that are available. I'll highlight a few. Very few jobs are so new that we don't know anything about them, so that a job process is already in many reference books.

Everyone wants to come in and *measure* what's in the environment, take air samples. It's a perfect gut reaction at first, but that's the worst way to go. It's the most difficult and the most expensive way. The best way would be to use reference texts on occupational health and occupational medicine—there are lay books and there are medical books that you could translate with a decent medical dictionary and look up the particular job. One book that is absolutely wonderful is called *Work is Dangerous To Your Health*. It's available in bookstores everywhere, and it lists different trades—if you're an electrical worker, you can look up what electrical workers are exposed to. The book also has a brief listing of the toxic effects of that particular exposure, so you can cross-reference in three or four different ways.

Another way to find out about toxins in your workplace is to contact the local Occupational Safety and Health Administration (OSHA).

Audience:

They are so understaffed you can't get help.

Dr. Miller:

You're right. The government agencies at this point are not much help; however they can be of help if they can provide information. In other words, call up with a specific question: "I want the NIOSH criteria document." There is an agency of the Federal government called NIOSH, the National Institute of Occupational Safety and Health. NIOSH is supposed to research safety and health matters, but has funneled that over to OSHA, the Occupational Safety and Health Administration which is the regulatory arm. OSHA is supposed to enforce the standards the NIOSH recommends. But NIOSH is involved in worker education and providing materials, and they have criteria documents. If you know if someone is exposed to a particular substance, these documents are available by writing or calling your local NIOSH area office. Call them and request the criteria document on benzine, or whatever it is you're interested in. That document has everything you ever wanted to know about the substance. Criteria documents are not available on every substance, but if it is a common exposure, it is available.

Also there are departments of occupational health and occupational medicine at universities from which you can request help. They run outpatient clinics where you can send people to be examined by professionals. Once you recognize symptoms or are suspicious, you ought to have that person evaluated by a professional who can diagnose a work-related illness, and who can take the work history in detail and find out whether exposures are related to the disease or problem that the person is having.

Audience:

I am particularly interested in large office buildings that are completely sealed; there is no fresh air coming in from anywhere and the air is constantly recirculated—when the circulators work. I'm working under those circumstances now. There are several hundred of us in a building that has no air circulation. We are wondering what recourse we have because we have trouble breathing. We have filed union complaints. We're county employees and we've even gone in front of the legislature, and we are still suffering.

Audience:

I know of a company with offices in a sealed building where there was no circulation of air and people suffered from breathing problems. The employees got in OSHA and forced the company to circulate air within the building.

Audience:

But we are government employees and it's very difficult to get OSHA to act.

Dr. Miller:

That's correct. Some government employees are not covered by OSHA, so you have one government agency suing another government agency and that creates all kinds of problems. In fact what you are referring to is common. They call it "tight building syndrome."

Audience:

Right. Mold grows on the walls from lack of air circulation.

Dr. Miller:

We have formaldehyde fumes coming off the drapes and the new carpeting. In new construction it's particularly a problem because you have all these synthetically-treated materials used in offices.

The common symptoms in tight building syndrome are mucous membrane irritation, eyes, nose and throat irritations, respiratory irritations, odors. Cigarette smoke is another problem in office buildings where the ventilation is poor or not circulated at all. In terms of mental health, a number of office employees who are having these symptoms thought they were crazy. Until they talked over their symptoms with other employees, they thought it was a particular weakness or problem that they were having.

Audience:

I've read about leakage of radiation from computers. I'm wondering whether leakage would constitute a hazard in a place that uses a great many high-power computers?

Dr. Miller:

What type of radiation? X-rays? Ionizing? Microwave radiation? There are so many kinds of radiation. Some mortality studies were done on workers who are exposed to high electrical current fields. The study looked at 10 or 11 different occupations: cable splicers, people who work on telephone poles, etc. The study found that in people who are exposed to high-power electrical fields there seems to be an excess of lymphatic and leukemic malignancies; this showed up in 10 of the 11 occupations studied. Perhaps that's the kind of electro-magnetic radiation you are referring to. Computers, to my knowledge, don't put out ionizing radiation, X-rays, the kinds of things you see in nuclear power plants or atomic facilities.

Audience:

Four cameramen with a major TV network have brain tumors and they claim the tumors are a result of the cameras which they held to their eyes.

Dr. Miller:

The stories we're hearing reinforce my theory that these are significant issues for people at work. I often feel that my own perspective is limited by the kind of people I continually see, but it is interesting to me that these problems are of everyday concern and are causing a lot of anxiety under the surface. Workers are looking around now and are suspicious of everything in the work environment and perhaps rightfully so. I often walk a very fine line between scaring people and informing them, between telling them this causes cancer and at the same time reassuring them that they're not going to be the one. From that, I see lots of mental health concerns.

Audience:

Is there a way to test the person if we can't test the environment?

Dr. Miller:

Yes, that's why I suggested the clinics where people are experienced at looking at an X-ray, or looking at a blood study, or looking at kidney function or liver function. The process that we use in occupational medicine is not very much different than any other form of medicine, except we focus on different things. I spend 80 percent of the time with my patients asking everything: every job they've ever had, what the exposures were on that job. I get what we call an occupational history, a full list of exposures and history. The reason the past is important is because the exposures of 20 years ago are the things we worry about, like cancer and chronic diseases, today. After the history process is done, I order the appropriate medical tests targeted toward the person's exposure and the expected resultant diseases related to that exposure.

Audience:

Isn't it the privilege of a company not to let people know what they've been exposed to? How in the world can you tell the clinic what you've been exposed to if you don't know?

Dr. Miller:

It's clearly a very crucial and difficult problem. That is why you see national and state-wide campaigns to pass right-to-know laws. It is one of the most difficult things that we face in diagnosis. Why shouldn't people know what they're working with and what the health hazards are and what they're exposed to? And yet, many industries in states without right-to-know laws retain that prerogative. In New York State there is a Right to Know law. As an employee in New York State, you can formally serve notice on your employer that you would like to know all the materials that are in use in this facility; whatever it is that you work with. The company must comply within 15 days or there is legal recourse. Some companies fight it. Companies often stonewall that request because the law is rather new and they're not used to having to give out that information.

Audience:

It seems that you can't always tell just from the work-place because the exposure could be interacting with the off-work place.

Dr. Miller:

Absolutely, which is why with a work history, we also inquire about hobbies and second jobs. This exterminator I was referring to had an extermination business on the side at home for extra income. We had to account for how much time he was spending and what was he using in the second job. So there are many compounding factors. But we must inquire—I'm sure many of you have been to physicians and never been asked where you work now, much less where you worked 20 years ago. It's not something that physicians are taught to ask, it's not something that they are tremendously concerned with. Their concerns are diagnosis and treatment. Our concerns are cause, etiology, and prevention.

You'd be surprised how creative individuals in a work-place can be. We've had people, for example, take the labels off of barrels; but even if it's a trade name there are books that can crack those trade names to find out what the chemical constituents are. There are material safety data sheets, which are sheets that come with the chemical or substance when it's purchased. Those sheets list the acute toxic effects, the things that are well known; you can't get it on your skin, it causes a rash, etc. The data sheets often don't say that it causes cancer, but they will often give you the chemical constituents. You can look up a trade name and find out the actual chemical identity. Many times when I ask an employee what chemicals he uses, he'll say, well I work with XL-40, or Lever Brothers 17. That doesn't help me very much, unless I crack those names by using the material safety data sheets. The data sheets are covered by the Right to Know law.

Audience:

I'd like to discuss confidentiality, particularly in terms of mental health.

Dr. Donheiser:

It's becoming more and more difficult to maintain confidentiality as the insurance companies demand more and more information. At one point, not too long ago, it was simply a matter of putting down on an insurance form, "nervous disorder," and that was readily accepted. Now, most insurance companies demand to know the *exact* diagnosis. What happens to that information once it gets to the insurance company is something, of course, that none of us knows. A lot of clerks handle it, it goes from hand to hand, it goes from desk to desk, through and around, and where it comes out, we just don't know. We don't have that much control over insurance companies.

We have control over the *information* we give to the insurance company, but again, the demands are getting greater for more highly specific information.

Dr. Winick:

One reason that a lot of workers come to the Central Labor Rehabilitation Council is they are afraid to have records of ailments on file at their own unions. What some unions have been able to do is require that the employer merely confirms that the employee was working during a particular period in question. A separate document with the details of the illness is sent directly to the insurance company and it is stipulated that the insurance company is never to share this with the employer.

Audience:

In my company, certain types of mental conditions are not allowed by contract to be paid and the benefits people have to call me to clarify why an employee is in the hospital. I've got to tell them.

Dr. Zoppa:

There is virtually no way in which an individual can maintain confidentiality as long as there is someone else paying the bill. If someone is out of work for several weeks, their employer wants to know where they have been. If they have been at a psychiatric hospital such as South Oaks Hospital, they obviously came here for either an emotional problem or a problem with substance abuse. Therefore, it's very hard to maintain confidentiality.

Audience:

I don't find that it's so much a stigma as far as the company is concerned. If the bosses know you were treated for alcoholism or cocaine abuse, that's okay, fine, as long as you have your act together now. That's what they look for.

Dr. Zoppa:

We hold back-to-work meetings prior to discharge with the patient and someone from his place of employment. We discuss what's been going on in therapy, how the patient has fared, where he or she stands right now, what the prospects are and what has to take place. This gives confidence to the patient and to the employer. The person knows that now important people at work are going to know what's going on and that he or she has done something to get help. Employers now know that help has been given and hopefully the employee will be a better worker.

Dr. Miller:

Are there any restrictions on what insurance companies do with information? Are there any laws or binding guidelines regarding the management who pays for the insurance policy? Also, what portion of management is entitled to that information? Sure, corporate medical needs to know, but does personnel? Should it not be a matter of confidentiality from physician to physician, from health care worker to health care worker? And should there be restrictions on what can be done with that information? Should we be focusing our efforts in terms of trying to pass regulations?

Dr. Winick:

In the labor movement in general, an absolute minimum of information is communicated. For example, if a business agent refers a member of his union to Central Labor Rehabilitation Council for treatment, he will not routinely be kept informed on the progress of the treatment. The employee will be asked if there is anybody he wishes us to notify that he is going into this treatment: if he says nobody, then nobody is notified of anything. Information is given on a need-to-know basis—only to the extent, if necessary, to protect the worker's job, to make representations on his behalf, to file a grievance on his behalf, or to follow-up on the outcome of treatment. Labor union management certainly prefers an absolute minimum communication. As far as I know, there's no body of law on this. It's a gray area.

Dr. Donheiser:

That's the problem. It's a gray area. There are Federal statutes governing the transmission of information regarding patients' privacy and confidentiality. There are state laws. The laws as far as I know, have specified the mode of transmission but only in certain limited areas. The rest of the areas are left vague and undefined. The company policies more or less determine how that information is used in the gray areas as opposed to the black and white areas.

Dr. Miller:

Do you mean to say that if I am a non-physician and if I write in to an insurance company that I want information on Frank Smith, that I don't need to demonstrate any reason to know?

Dr. Donheiser:

There is no law that specifically states what happens to that insurance form once it reaches the desk of the receiving clerk at the insurance company. The receiving clerk goes through that insurance form and decides whether it is an allowable claim, and then puts it in the hands of the next clerk who determines how much is to be paid. Then it's handed to the next clerk in the payment department, and then the next clerk in some other department. So on and so on.

Audience:

As a private practitioner not concerned with the delicacies of the desires of the insurance company or the employer, and also as one who four years ago gave up supporting malpractice insurance companies, I'm liable to suit. So I take care. Now, when I get a request from the patient to give a report, I have to have written specific permission to give that report, and with recognition that I have no responsibility for what happens. Incidentally, I don't mail the report, I give it to the patient. Well, so far, I've had no trouble but I've been practicing only 50 years, I may still get in trouble. I wish I had the money I've given to the malpractice insurance all those years.

One thing I will put in the report, however, is if the patient's condition is such, or the medication he is taking is such as to make it dangerous for him to handle delicate machinery, or to drive, I will always include that no matter how the patient may kick about it. I think that is my responsibility in giving that report.

Dr. Miller:

I agree. Do you have your own release form that you've developed, your own authorization form which includes all these specifics?

Audience:

No. It's on an individual basis. And if there are any questions concerning the patient's reliability or accountability, then a member of his or her family must sign it, as well as the patient.

Dr. Zoppa:

The physician, as the result of third-party payments, has been put in a very difficult position. Part of the Hippocratic oath is that information is kept confidential. With third party payment, that's gone by the boards. Physicians are forced to give material to insurance companies or they won't get paid. What happens with the material afterwards, they have no control over. Hopefully if it's a corporation they'll keep it within the medical department and not give it to personnel.

Chapter 4

THE ROLE OF THE OCCUPATIONAL HEALTH NURSE WITH THE FAMILY

Jeanne T. Healey, R.N., M.A.

If the physical and emotional health of the family is to become an integral part of a health care program in the workplace, it is necessary to look at the responsibility of the occupational health nurse for delivering that care.

Prior to retirement, Ms. Healey was Nursing Service Director, on the staff of the Corporate Medical Director, at Western Electric Company. A graduate of a three-year diploma program in nursing, Ms. Healey holds a B.S. degree and an M.A. degree in Nursing Education from Teacher's College, Columbia University. A Certified Occupational Health Nurse, Ms. Healey is a founding member of the original certification board. Her nursing experience includes both hospital and military service. She served as a nursing instructor and as a consultant to the New York City Department of Health. For 10 years, Ms. Healey was a part-time lecturer at the New York University School of Environmental Health, and has also held positions as staff nurse, supervising nurse, and consultant through the years. Ms. Healey has contributed numerous articles to both nursing and company publications, and with Western Electric, conducted a detailed study for assessment and utilization of company nurses. Findings from this study led to expanded nursing functions and extensive in-service education programs within the company.

Reflecting back on my early years as a nurse (when the title was industrial nurse), I am reminded of the various roles assigned to me—roles that were procedure-oriented, and limited only to the care of the employee. How often I was reminded of my limitations as defined in a job description written by someone other than a nurse. The frustration of these limitations, however, was a key factor in the development of an objective that carried over to the end of my career: my goal was to change the image of the nurse.

I found that it was—and still is—necessary to convince management, physicians, and unions of the true value of the occupational health nurse. I would like to talk about some of my successes and failures, and make some predictions for the future of the nurse who works in industry.

Nursing leaders in the field have spent much time and effort trying to define a specific role for the nurse yet, invariably, non-medical personnel are charged with the responsibility of writing a nursing job description. Nurses should describe their own job functions. I believe that a good job description should hold the nurse responsible for planning and implementing programs that include the family, both directly and indirectly. A job description that does this is the beginning of expanded functions for the nurse.

Experience has taught me that there is no worker, whether blue collar or white collar, who leaves family problems at home when he or she arrives at the workplace. It follows then that if we are to expect efficient production from a satisfied worker, we must think in terms of programs that help workers' families.

I recall the first nursing supervisor I had, and her advice about the family. While orienting me in the procedure of taking pre-employment histories, she suggested that I start out, not with routine questions, but by asking the candidate to tell me about his or her family. It seemed to work, and I learned early of the importance of the family.

There is also the responsibility to the family from a management viewpoint. In today's economy, management is bearing a heavy burden with costs for health insurance, disability payments, and Workers' Compensation. Unions and the government are demanding better health care for workers on the job, yet individuals are forced to cope with the stress of family problems on their own, without the help of unions or management.

I believe management has a responsibility to help families, but as strongly as I feel about the responsibility, I believe we must look at the situation realistically in terms of costs and results. New programs must be justified in terms of need. Any expansion of the health program will cost money and personnel. Why not make use of the resources management already has by using nursing personnel to implement programs that will help to fill at least some of the needs of the worker and the family?

Before I can talk about programs, I'd like to touch briefly on stress and the distressed employee.

We live in a society where pressures and problems at times seem insurmountable. Values tend to change almost as rapidly as technology. What are some of the stress situations that the occupational health nurse must deal with? Absenteeism probably heads the list and is a major concern for management. There was a time when home visits to absent employees were part of the company nurse's job. I was one of those nurses. The purpose of the home visit was to validate the illness and confirm that the employee was under adequate medical care. Involvement with the

worker's family was perhaps the most important outcome
of these visits.

Several years later, I was to participate in a cost and
effect study of the program and it was decided, except for
selected cases, to discontinue the home visits. They were
replaced by a formal, well-defined telephone visitation
program. The effect of the telephone program on absenteeism was difficult to evaluate, but an important objective
was accomplished—contact with the family of the employee, and the opportunity to offer further help if needed.
All contacts were documented in a report to the personnel
office, but details of the telephone counseling, unless job-
related, remained confidential.

Alcoholism and drug abuse are two of the major fam-
ily-related problems seen in industry today, yet few industries fully utilize the nurse in existing programs. It has
been my experience that the nurse is often the first person
to suspect an early drinking problem. Her statistics are
usually higher than those known to management. She
should be held responsible for early detection, referral for
treatment, and program planning involving workers and
their families.

Health education programs provide an excellent opportunity for family involvement. Nurses have always done
health education, but usually on a one-to-one basis. A program that we planned and implemented at Western Electric
was designed to reach the majority of employees and their
families.

At each company location, one nurse was designated
as the Health Education Coordinator, and was responsible
for all health education programs. Health fairs, open to
the family, were held that included screenings for early
detection of diseases, and literature aimed at the family.
One location developed a questionnaire asking for sug-
gestions from the family. The results were used in future

programs. Health education programs can be held during lunchtime or after working hours to reduce cost by avoiding time away from work for participants.

Illness of a family member can't help but cause anxiety and stress for a worker. Some years ago, we offered a program to teach home nursing care to employees who might have someone at home with a long-term critical disabling illness. With the assistance of the American Red Cross, our company nurses taught a home nursing course at the workplace after hours. To our surprise, the employees enrolled were both male and female, all having a need to take care of a sick or diabled family member. The demand for the course extended for about two years, and we were gratified with such success.

It is hardly necessary to say that the occupational health nurse is seeing the stresses resulting from divorce, family separation, homosexuality, and the anxiety of working mothers. There are few who haven't seen the anxiety associated with retirement. Some of this retirement anxiety could be lessened by offering pre-retirement counseling to employees and spouses, and nurses should be given responsibility for these pre-retirement health sessions.

In the majority of industries today, direct medical services to the family seem highly improbable. But until this becomes a reality, we must reach the family indirectly through planned programs. Those I have mentioned are but a few avenues. It is important to note, however, that *counseling* by the nurse is an integral part of any plan to reach the family.

Unfortunately, counseling *per se* is not taught in the majority of nursing schools. For this reason, I'd like to see management and physicians provide some type of training in counseling skills which would encourage the nurse to recognize and counsel the distressed employee. We did this at Western Electric. With the approval of upper management, we conducted a fairly successful counseling program for nurses.

The geographical distribution of company nurses made it impossible to conduct classes at all locations, but through the use of company facilities, we were able to produce a series of videotapes that could be circulated among locations.

Our objective was to provide information on counseling techniques, attitudes, and particularly listening skills. Although each tape had a specific topic, no formal script was used. Situational role-playing (followed by discussion) was used as the major teaching tool. After a group of nurses watched the tape, a telephone conference was held with the corporate psychiatrist to allow for further discussion. As serious, formal counseling began to take hold, nurses were encouraged to seek help, via telephone, from Dr. Howard Hess, the corporate psychiatrist.

What were the basic skills emphasized in the program? A counselor must have a sincere interest in the client, but must also understand that the purpose of counseling is not to change the person, but to allow him to recognize problems and cope with whatever resources he has at his command.

Emphasis was placed on developing the ability to do wholehearted *listening* by centering attention on the client. Nurses were advised to resist the temptation to tell or advise the employee what to do. (Basic nursing taught us just the opposite.) We stressed the need to do counseling in a quiet room, by appointment, and with time limits made known to the client.

Nurses were advised to assure the employee that information imparted would be confidential and would not be held against him in the work situation. Details of the sessions were not charted, but case reports were sent to the corporate psychiatrist for evaluation. Nurses were encouraged to develop a list of resources for referral of employees who needed assistance and/or care beyond which they were qualified to offer.

The intent of the counseling course was not to make professional counselors out of all nurses, but rather to create an awareness of the growing number of employees in need of help. Our efforts were aimed at providing a foundation for the nurse to offer that help.

It is my fondest hope that all nurses will recognize the importance of counseling and seek out educational opportunities that will strengthen their skills. I'd like to see a qualified nurse counselor in the medical unit of every occupational setting. I'd like to see the nurse working hand-in-hand with community resources, particularly with social agencies and with public health nurses.

In every job description for an occupational health nurse, I would like to see the responsibility for health education programs that include the family.

I'd like to see industry give more thought to the problems of working mothers. I'd like to see child care facilities provided at the workplace, using the valuable services of retired men and women. I can't begin to remember how many mothers I have known who forfeit vacation days because of baby-sitter problems. That causes stress, and stress causes problems at work.

To further extend my hopes for the future, I would like to see family clinics established where physical and emotional care is sponsored by industry. A comparative cost study of such care versus payments made through insurance plans might yield some interesting results. I sincerely hope that industry will, in the future, and without pressure from the government, see fit to extend health services to the family of the worker.

It is an exciting era in occupational medicine, and I foresee occupational nursing assuming more and more responsibility for total care of the worker. I believe this will happen if nurses are relieved of "roles" that lesser-trained personnel could perform. With support from management and physicians, I believe that occupational health nurses are willing, through their known flexibility, to assume responsibility for involvement with the family of the worker.

SELECTED READING

Baughn, S.L. The Role of the Nurse in Dealing with Stress in the Industrial Setting, April 1976. Journal of Occupational Nursing, 24(4): 15

Brown, M.L. The Extended Role of the Nurse in Occupational Mental Health Programs. December 1971. Industrial Medicine and Surgery, 19-13

Lee, J.A., The New Nurse In Industry. U.S. Dept. of Health, Education, and Welfare. January 1978. Public Health Service. Cincinnati, Ohio.

Salatti, R.A. The Occupational Health Nurse as a Mental Health Counselor. December 1976. Journal of Occupational Health Nursing, 25(12): 23

Secretary's Committee to Study Extended Roles for Nurses. Extending the Scope of Nursing Practice. Report of the Secretary's Committee to Study Extended Roles for Nurses. 1971. D.H.E.W. Publication No. 73-2037. U.S. Government Printing Office. Washington, D.C.

DISCUSSION

Chaired by speaker Ms. Healey, this panel included: Virginia Accetta, R.N., M.S., Clinical Specialist, Outpatient Department, University Hospital at Stony Brook; Marie

Arprano, R.N., M.S., Clinical Specialist, Consultation and Liaison Service, University Hospital at Stony Brook; John J. Dowling, M.D., M.P.H., Commissioner, Nassau County Department of Health; and Jacqueline Rose Hott, R.N., Ph.D., F.A.A.N., Executive Director, Mid Atlantic Regional Nursing Association.

Ms. Healey:

Do you have any particular problems that you would like answers for? One of the thoughts that occurred to me was how comfortable is the nurse in dealing with a worker's sexual problems.

Audience:

As a nurse, the avenue of sexual problems that I encounter is related to medication. A lot of people who are prescribed hypertension medications stop taking them because they affect sexual ability. I counsel them to go back to their doctor and see about a change in medication. I'd like to have more insight into the problem.

Dr. Hott:

What I'm seeing in business, on the job, is that sexuality just doesn't stop in the bedroom. We're sexual beings wherever we are, so that on the job, what we think of ourselves as sexual beings is going to come out. The problem of medications—whether they be for high blood pressure, depression, diabetes—is that, in general, medicines may have anywhere from almost no physical impact in terms of sexual function to a great deal of emotional impact. There are rules that I'm sure many of you have heard in terms of medication that relate to sexual functioning, and that is either change the dose, change the medication, or change the physician. It's difficult as a nurse in industry, or the nurse in the school, or the nurse in the coronary

care unit to begin to suggest that, but we must at least begin
to have the patient made aware that many people are ex-
periencing similar difficulties. We must give our patients
permission to discuss problems.

In many coronary care units, the nurses have to wait
for the doctor's permission to discuss anything relating to
sexual adjustment. That may be the last thing that's told
to a patient, and it's told in a pamphlet given them as they
leave. Many of the nurses in coronary care units—in fact,
many of us nurses *anywhere*—feel uncomfortable in dealing
with anything relating to sexual function. And many doctors will say, "I don't want the nurse to discuss it. I will
discuss it when the patient comes back for the visit." In
terms of the occupational health nurse, the patient probably hasn't gone back to work yet, but sex is an activity of
daily living, just as going back to work is an activity of daily
living. The spouse, or the significant other, whoever it is
that that patient is concerned about in terms of sexual
functioning, is just as worried about returning to a normal
activity of daily living as far as a job, as far as food, as far
as sex, as far as anything else. Somewhere along the line,
the nurse—whether in industry, or in the coronary unit—
is the one who can detect and predict what the problems
are going to be.

Just a word about sexuality. Many of us feel that it is
not appropriate for us to talk about sexuality. It's for
somebody else to talk about. If you feel that way, then it's
not appropriate for you to talk about, but it is necessary
for you to know to whom you can refer questions to, someone who *is* comfortable talking about it. But the first point
is to give permission to the patient and the family to feel
that it's OK to talk about it; they don't have to be ashamed
and they don't have to hide. Use your declarative statements, such as: "Many men say that, after taking Indoral,
this is what happens," or, "Many women say that after hys-

terectomy, they feel very uncomfortable during sex." That's the opening, that gives your patients permission to feel that way.

Dr. Dowling:
I'd like to comment on that from a slightly different perspective. For years, my department has been involved in a hypertensive community screening program. One observation we made after evaluating our first four to five years with the program was that our main problem with hypertensive patients was not in identifying those who did not know that they had the disease, but with those who *knew* they had it—and their physicians knew they had it—but were not taking their medicines. So if the reason is that taking the medicines interferes with their sexual functioning, then it's certainly something that must be brought out into the open.

Ms. Accetta:
It occurred to me that the occupational health nurse literally has her finger on the pulse of what's going on in that company with those workers. With the knowledge of things such as the family life cycle and the number of single parent families—women more than men running single parent families—and the knowledge of all the various stages of the life cycle, the occupational health nurse is in a wonderful position to provide people with a tremendous amount of preventive help or at least early intervention. If someone comes in with hypertension or a variety of somatic complaints and you take a history that indicates that this person is under a large amount of stress, you're in a good position then to provide stress management programs.
The occupational nurse should be sitting in on the planning committee, so that anytime there's a change made

in the work environment or in the organizational chart, or anytime people are going to be laid off, she knows about it. Because change is stressful.

The nurse is prepared to sit on any committee and have some kind of liaison with management and planning so that she can identify high risk employees and then influence management and plan programs.

Dr. Hott:

Are you aware of a National Institute for Occupational Safety and Health (NIOSH) study that indicated the cost-effectiveness of having an occupational health nurse on staff? It seems to be one of the best-kept secrets in industry.

Audience:

I'd like to address a problem that I've come across in my work as an occupational health nurse at an air traffic control center. A high percentage of controllers are men, and they have, in passing, mentioned sexual problems to me. Not extensive conversations, though, and the reason is they just don't have the time. They have been working a six-day week, and I run into problems setting up health programs. First of all, to have any programs after working hours is out of the question—they just want to go home. To have a program during working hours is hard—they cannot be relieved in order to come to a program. The controllers only have one day off a week, and it's beginning to show. There is an increase in hypertension, they are irritable, they don't want to take the time out to come to the medical department. If they do get a few free minutes they want to run to the cafeteria and get a cup of coffee.

Ms. Healey:

You might think in terms of calling in an expert to help you plan seminars on sexual dysfunction or stress, or whatever you feel to be the greatest need of these men. You may have to plan it six months or a year in advance. By the time you justify it, and by the time you decide what are the most important factors that you want to have covered, it will take that long.

Ms. Accetta:

There are a few things I've learned in terms of dealing with organizations, and one way you may get cooperation in formulating an education program is to get statistics. That makes an impact. One of the things that you may do is start collecting your own statistics; keep a record of when the changes happen within the company and date how many people you see for hypertension, how many people you see for ulcers, etc. Then you have some kind of report. You have statistics which can be of vital interest to anyone who is trying to decide what kind of stresses this job places on people. If you want to offer a program, say, in stress reduction, the company is bound to ask you what you have to back up this need. I would encourage any of you who want to make an impact on the place where you work to start collecting your own statistics—even if no one tells you to do it. Even if the statistics are crude or rough, you can make an impact.

Dr. Hott:

It will be important for you to have statistics on how many pregnant husbands you have. One of my areas of research has been on the stresses of the first-time father. Certainly you are aware that this is one of the most stressful times in a man's life, as his responsibility increases. Some of the results of my research have also shown that there are physical changes in the male during the pregnancy, as well as the psychological changes. Because of this stress, fertility problems can increase.

This is a time of increased responsibility. The beginning of a family, the new family, the increases in family are very difficult and stressful times. How can the occupational health nurse reach out to say it's OK to talk about these problems?

How many of you are involved in any kind of parent education groups?

Ms. Healey:

This is a very simple thing to carry out in a simple way in industry. I've seen parent education done at lunch time by a nurse. She would round up as many pregnant women as she could—she did not include fathers, that was back five or six years—and get them all to bring their lunch, sit around a conference table and talk. It was amazing how much education she could do during lunch. If you can't do that, do you have a place in the community where you can send employees for parent education?

Dr. Hott:

Excellent resources to industry are schools of nursing and institutions within your community. There are many maternity services within hospitals where students from local universities are doing their maternity practicum; these students would be interested, with a call from the occupational health nurse, to help develop such a program.

Thinking about the traffic controller situation, a frequent concern of the worker is that there is no time for sex. They're tired when they get home. It's always the last thing that's done after putting out the cat and watching Johnny Carson. It's the last of the priorities so there's never any time. You have to go back to the worker with a self-care approach. When do your workers say *is* a good time? When do *they* see there might be time? Ask them about planning within their schedule.

Ms. Healey:

What about the request for sex information from teenagers? Are you getting requests? I know that they are not getting good information in high school. I am absolutely floored at how little these kids know. They may have problems that they want to discuss with you, and they may be very legitimate questions. They're not all as worldly as they pretend to be.

Ms. Arprano:

I never really looked at myself as an occupational nurse but I suddenly realized I do a lot of occupational nursing. I work in a hospital with a lot of women, nurses, who have a lot of problems and frequently the problems are manifested in patient care. What I deal with is staff problems, acting out, absenteeism, anger, difficulty with peer relationships. And I understand the time problem—nurses don't have time for themselves. So what I do is get into work early in the morning, during change of shift, and talk to two shifts at one time, trying not to use much time. If nurses know they're obligated for an hour, they say it's impossible; they look at their schedules and know they cannot take the hour. But by making the demands on their time modest, you get more than you bargain for.

Dr. Dowling:

One of the problems of helping is knowing and keeping track of the changing resources. However, there are resources within resources which can direct you where to go if you have a problem. One of those is the information and referral service which we recently reorganized. We are putting more stress on information rather than referral. Prior to the reorganization, the emphasis was on referral. People calling in with problems are now being directed to other sources for help. We respond to questions as well as refer to the appropriate resource. The telephone number for this service is listed under the Nassau County Department of Health, Information and Referral. We would take your questions about parent-teacher classes, family health services, communication, family planning, or many of the other resources that exist and put you in touch with the appropriate individual or agency, hopefully guide you in contacting them for appropriate follow-through.

In Nassau County, we also have a group of public health nurses who have responsibility for development of prevention and promotion activities within their geographic service areas. We have divided the county into four service areas. If you're in industry, and your particular plant falls within the catchment areas of one of the health centers, there are individuals now assigned to each area, who would be willing to discuss your needs and discuss the services available to you. If it is parenting classes you want, or sex education classes, there is a group of nurses who have the training and experience to help you organize classes, whether you wish to conduct them yourselves, or have one of the public health nurses conduct them. All you have to do there is call the health center within the catchment area where your industry is located.

We've been talking about prospective fathers. Relating that to toxic chemicals, in the past, most of the concern has been with regard to the impact of toxic chemicals upon women. There is recognition lately that the effect of toxic chemicals on the male sperm may produce a deleterious affect on the embryo's development. Again, in Nassau County, there are at least two resources available which have the staff and the technology to follow through on this problem. They are North Shore University Hospital and the Nassau County Medical Center. To repeat, we are interested, we're concerned, and we'd be willing to work with you as individuals or as a group with regard to your problems. All you have to do is call us.

Dr. Hott:

I would also note that we are comparatively rich on Long Island with educational institutions that can also provide consulting services: Stony Brook University, Suffolk County Community College, Adelphi, Post, Farmingdale, Nassau Community College. They all have faculty who are prepared in community health nursing, and many of them have the resources to work specifically in terms of occupational health nursing. So I would ask you to use those resources as well.

It's also an area that is fertile for those of you who want to be consultants to industry, in terms of setting up your individual practices. You have the right under the nurse-practice act in New York State to do this as health promotion, health teaching, health counseling.

Audience:

I work for an insurance company in a job that is a continuation of the occupational health role in the workplace, but I go into the home. I interview the patient or the injured worker, I act as a liaison between the patient, the doctor, and the company. My role in working for the insurance company is to give the best possible care to the patient while looking at costs. We set up help in the home if the patient needs it, we set up necessary equipment. We can go into the hospital and get the patient out of the hospital faster by setting up the equipment they need at home and this cuts hospital costs. It's better for the patient; he's in the home environment. We also look to the needs of the family. I want to stress that we're not investigators. Our first allegiance is to the patient. We are nurses and very professional. We do counseling, and one-to-one health teaching; we refer to the proper agencies. When there's a problem in the home, we can do some rather grandiose things at times. I had a patient one time who needed help in the home. We called her mother in from France. It was excellent for the patient's mental health. They had a nice visit, the mother supplied the home care, the insurance company saved money, and everybody was happy.

Audience:

I am an occupational health consultant. I would suggest that occupational health nurses tour their own companies. You can learn an awful lot about your plant. Go around with surveyors. They'll be willing to explain their sampling techniques and how the lab will analyze the data, and what the results will mean to you.

Dr. Dowling:

I'd like to know if you, as nurses, feel comfortable dealing with the workers and their families, that is, becoming involved in the individual's family problems in the work setting.

How do you keep the information confidential? Do you keep it within your own shop, or does it become part of the personnel record?

Audience:

I'd like to tell you how I handle confidentiality in a school. My staff is mostly an older group. They are trying to hang on to their jobs, but they're being pressured into early retirement, by young teachers who need the jobs to support growing families. So, if the older teacher is having a medical problem, and comes to talk to me in the nurse's office, they tell me "Don't put it in my file, don't tell the administrators." If a teacher is pregnant, she won't tell anybody until she begins to show. Meanwhile she's still teaching the classes. She thinks someone will presssure her to take a maternity leave, and she'll be excessed. I don't share with the administration some of the things that are told to me unless teaching is affected—I usually find out from students if there are problems in the classroom because the kids are first to tell me.

Confidentiality is the focus. Where is your allegiance as a nurse? To your patient? I walk that tightrope with my teenage girls, also. Do I tell their parents that they're pregnant or they've had an abortion or do I just keep that confidential? It's a fence that's not easy to straddle.

Dr. Hott:

It's a serious moral and ethical problem that we all face. We are also employees. What would we want done with our own records? What's the confidentiality that we want protected? To whom do those records belong? Do they belong to us, to the employer, or to the insurance company? I've had couples who've come to me who decided not to use their insurance benefits because they did not want a report going back to the insurance company saying there was a sexual dysfunction. And the same with psychiatric problems as well. It is a fine line, and one needs the support of colleagues. We really have to feel strength within ourselves in terms of saying whatever decision I make is the right one.

Ms. Accetta:

I'd like to underline what Dr. Hott said. I've had families come to me who were having a problem with their children; the parents did not want to file for insurance benefits because they felt that even though their *kids* were having a problem, that could somehow be used against them at work situation. That was kind of astonishing to me. But from my frame of reference, problems at work often result because of children's problems. First the parents may be holding things together pretty well, but the kid experiences the stress and the kid starts drinking, acting out, being truant from school, a whole variety of things.

Audience:

When I go out to see a patient, I establish an excellent rapport with the family. If it's a man who has been injured, I work closely with his wife. Which brings up a point: the *wife* will talk to me about sexual problems. Sometimes, but not usually, the husband will. An injured woman will talk about sex. I can refer for help or just listen; sometimes they just want a listening ear.

If I talk about a personal problem, I will allude in my report to a personal problem but no specifics. It's nobody's business. If that patient tells me they don't want that talked about, that's between the patient, the wife, and myself. We will try to work things out. How I work things out doesn't matter to the insurance company. You have to protect your patient. That's why you fight to the end to protect them.

Dr. Dowling:

If I may ask another question of the group: What do you think about programs at the work site which relate to behavior modification? These programs are sponsored by the employers, with the support of employees and their union.

Audience:

We had a pilot program which we sent out questionnaires to a selective group asking about their interests and concerns. Stress on the job was a prime concern. We held two sessions, with four nurses, on the subject. The employees came on their lunch hour, and it was very successful. We're now in the process of volunteering some of the other nurses to do any form of teaching that they feel they may be able to do with their captive audience. So it is possible. I foresee that we'll be doing a variety of programs.

Dr. Hott:

There are at least four major employers in New York City that have done this recently. So there's a precedent of employers who are offering programs, stress reduction and relaxation management to their employees. They offer them at lunch time or on breaks and they are very useful programs.

Ms. Accetta:

Again, if you can collect some statistics and get yourself involved in committees and planning and so forth, you can get the backing of the management which says we will allow an hour off to our employees in order for them to attend these meetings.

We need some kind of clout within our companies and I would urge you to get to know your company well and find out what the bottom line is. It's usually money. If you can find some way of showing that, through stress reduction, or pre-divorce counseling, or whatever, you can prevent absenteeism or illness, then you're going to have some clout. Make yourselves knowledgeable on that and get yourselves on some committees.

Audience:

Our company conducted a behavior modification program for smoking cessation. Over a period of two years, we provided group counseling for smoking cessation; it was discontinued only because we reached every employee in the compnay who was willing, or at all interested, in quitting smoking. We reduced our smoking population by something like 55 percent during those two years.

Ms. Healey:

Suppose you want to put on a smoking cessation program two years from now. Are you going to be able to say to management—suppose you have a new management at that point—here are the results of the last program?

Audience:

The results are well documented. We have an employee education department within our medical division which handles all of those procedures.

Audience:

We've been talking about all the programs that we, as occupational health nurses, can provide for our employees. Does management know about providing programs for nurses? Do companies give nurses the time to go for continuing education? Are they aware that continuing education hours are mandatory? Do our employers give *us* the time?

Audience:

One of the bones of contention is always that since we are professionals we should take our own time to attend many of these ongoing educational programs. Then again, everybody has to function on the reality base. Besides your job, there are many other facets of your life, too, and should you be spending your vacation time with your family instead of attending week-long seminars?

Dr. Hott:

You should really look at it as a condition of employment. Just as you look at any of the benefits that you are going to get when you take the job, whether it's medical benefits or vacation time. What are your educational benefits? What are the benefits that accrue to you if you go on for a master's degree or if you go on for a doctorate? What tuition remittance do you get? What are the points you earn for attending a seminar? Even though continuing education is *not* mandatory in New York, what does it mean to your company that you're here today? What will it mean in terms of a salary increment? Of days off? This is part of our bargaining position. You're a valued asset to industry, and I think we as nurses—and as a profession that is 97 percent female—have to begin to assert our value and our self-worth. When we're looking for a job and we know that we're valued in that job, we speak for ourselves.

Chapter 5

MANAGEMENT'S VIEW
OF THE PROBLEM

Leon Warshaw, M.D.

Leon J. Warshaw, M.D., is Executive Director of the New York Business
Group on Health, a coalition working for cost-effective health care. From
1967 through 1980, he was Vice President and Corporate Medical Director
of the Equitable Life Assurance Society. Dr. Warshaw is a Board-certified
internist and maintained a practice in internal medicine and cardiology.
He is also certified in occupational medicine and was Medical Director of
Paramount Pictures Corp., United Artists Corp., and American Broadcasting
Company. He has served as a consultant on employee health management
to a broad range of industrial organizations and governmental agencies.
He is a graduate of Columbia College and Columbia University's College
of Physicians and Surgeons, and has held faculty positions at a number
of universities. Dr. Warshaw is presently a clinical professor of environmental medicine at New York University and is on the consulting staff of
the Center for Industry and Health Care at Boston University. For two and
a half years, he was a loaned executive assigned as Deputy Director for
Health Affairs of the New York Mayor's Office of Operations. Dr. Warshaw
has been reappointed for a second three-year term as a member of the
New York Governor's Health Advisory Council. He has published over 200
contributions to professional journals, and three books including *The Heart
in Industry* and *Managing Stress*. Dr. Warshaw has been elected a fellow
of many prestigious professional societies and has served on a number
of advisory boards.

Selecting me for this last spot on the program raises some questions. First, think of it in terms of a manager of a baseball team. Who's the last hitter in the batting order? The fellow with the lowest average. On the other hand, my background in show biz tells me that you always save the big star for the last one in the performance. That really set me up fine until I started thinking of a parade. Who's the last person down the street in the parade? The fellow with the broom and the shovel, and you know what he deals with. There's a point to that story, however: the matter of perspective.

We are looking at mental health in its inordinate complexity and we're looking at industry in its inordinate complexity. And we're putting both together in a rapidly changing world and a rapidly changing environment fraught with all kinds of problems and tensions. We must never lose track of those complexities. There's a tendency in meetings of this kind to put things in terms of generalities and platitudes. In the hands of experts, these quickly become jargon. And I'll be guilty of that; I must warn you against it. It's the old story of whether the glass is half-full or half-empty, the fable of the blind men and the elephant. It's a matter of perspective.

I must warn you also against the tubular vision of expert, and the doctrinaire viewpoints of the evangelist. There are many perspectives.

At this point, let me insert a perspective of The New York Business Group on Health. We are a newly-formed, rapidly growing coalition of employers in the greater New York area who are concerned about the availability, quality, and affordability of health care. We have a special class of membership for providers of health services, and I am pleased that South Oaks Hospital was one of the first hospitals to join.

The Group pursues a broad range of activities through

task forces, seminars, conferences, workshops, publications, and research and demonstration projects. All are focused on controlling health care costs and, more importantly in the long run, eliminating the need for health services by preventing illness and disability. We monitor health policy issues, the legislative and regulatory activities of government on all levels, and the behavior of the providers of health services.

In looking back over the field of mental health and industry to see how far we've come, I noticed that, so far, no one at this meeting has talked about mental illness. We've talked about mental health. Have we eradicated mental illness? We have not—it remains very much a problem, even though we don't talk about it. For the sake of the record, let's remember that it does exist, that there are psychiatric illnesses. Let's note for the record that people do recover and let's say that it's perfectly good business to hire individuals who have recovered. All of us as mental health professionals work for their rehabilitation and their reabsorption into their jobs and society. I think that needed to be said.

Now, a second point of clarification is needed about the concept of the hazards of the workplace, about the dehumanizing effects of work. These exist and they are very real. But again, let's keep our perspective and recognize that work is an essential part of living, certainly in our society; that work is therapeutic; that one of the reasons why retirement and loss of job is so hazardous is actually the deprivation of work.

I recently had the opportunity to be in mainland China. There is no unemployment in China. Everybody who's politically acceptable is on the payroll. I talked to a young man who'd been at work in a particular career as an electrical something-or-other—everybody in China is an electrician. (Good heavens, anybody who's been there would hope that they would train a few *plumbers*.) He'd been working on his job for two years. I said, "What do you do?" He said, "I haven't done anything yet. They assigned me to this job in this factory and the factory hasn't been built yet." He'd been drawing a salary for two years. Underemployment is a terribly demoralizing problem. It's not as bad as total unemployment when you don't have the economic sustenance of the earnings, but it is in itself a very significant problem.

Now, let's get some definitions in order. My charge is to talk about the management. What is management? Are we talking about management from the standpoint of large companies? What about all of the smaller companies in the growing number of industrial parks? And what about the husband and wife who, with perhaps three or four part-time employees, run a very significant enterprise where people work?

When we talk about management, I think we have to recognize that there will be different perceptions from the standpoint of the different types of organization of what management is, does, or can do. We have to think in terms of the expertise of the people whom we dignify by designating them as management. Are they professionals in human relations, in personnel work, in medical care, in counseling, in nursing? Or simply M.B.A.'s or accountants or executives of one sort or another? What about their closeness to the workers for whom they're responsible? When I say closeness, I mean social level, socio-economic level, geographic level.

What is their relationship to the workers? Is it that of a peer, that of a supervisor? Don't forget that the union representative is also a manager. How much time does the manager have to concern himself about employees' concerns and needs? In a company like Western Electric, there are experts who are brought in either on a salaried level or as consultants to deal with these problems. But how about the small business manager who, in this day and age, is spending every hour of every day worrying about interest rates, if his supplier is getting the materials to him, the shipping of his products, his customer relations—in all, really keeping the business alive and afloat? When does he or she have time to deal with people problems?

What's the point of concern of the manager? That's very often determined by the position of the individual, either in terms of assignment in level, or in terms of time; and these change from day to day. Is it workers' health? Is it productivity? Work performance? Absenteeism? Is it disruption in the workplace? Is it the cost of health benefits? Any and all of these. So when we speak of management's interest and management's concern, and management's responsibility, we have to address these varying viewpoints.

And we have to think in terms of the balance between concern on the one hand and the ability in terms of expertise, time, and resources to deal with it.

Now my title is also, "Management's View of the Problem." What's the problem? I've talked to some managers who say, "There is no problem. We have no problem with the mental health of our employees, or indeed with the health of our employees. We're all just a happy family." (As far as I'm concerned, the family may be one of the most combative war zones imaginable.)

A second response one gets from managers is, "It's none of my business. This is the private life of the employee, the private life of the family, and I, as an employer, have no right to intrude."

Indeed, there are some workers and some unions who would say, "Right on. That's *our* business. All you have to do is be sure we get paid for what we do, and let us worry about the rest."

Another answer is—and this is a harder one to get; it's only after you begin to talk to managers that they will reveal this—the real answer is, "I don't want to get involved, because the minute I show some interest in this, the people are going to say I'm doing this because I have a guilty conscience, that it's all my fault. If I get involved, it would be an admission of guilt."

Of course, a great cop-out is to say, "It's a community responsibility; I'm a small businessman—or I'm a large businessman—and it's not my business to look after these problems. This is a problem for government, this is a problem for the voluntary agency, this a problem for the church, the community, and so on."

Indeed it is, in part, but it's also a business responsibility.

Of course, there's the age-old comment one hears from managers and supervisors which goes, "As long as the employee gets his work done, as long as he reports on the job and turns in a reasonable day for it, that's all that matters." But we all know about the weekend alcoholic, or the "recreational use" of drugs, or the intrusion of family problems that the worker can't leave at the plant gate, but inevitably brings into the work site.

One of the most pervasive answers I think, and one of the most discouraging, is the acknowledgement that there *is* a problem—that everything's wrong. And of course, the problem is compounded when we not only think in terms of the workplace, but we think of government and regulations, unions, the problems that are thrust upon us by minorities, by blacks, by women, by young, by old, by failure of the criminal justice system and all of that. So we hear, "There's so much that's wrong, that I'm powerless. There's nothing I can do about it. And why even begin to try?"

Another common response: "It is a problem, but I can't

afford to deal with it globally. I can worry about it in terms of my key people, my executives, or relatives of mine that I happen to have on the payroll. I can only worry about myself. I can only worry about my long-term employees who've been with me for so long a time that they've earned some loyalty and consideration on my part. But why should I knock myself out for people who are not going to be with me next year or the year after?"

Another common response: "It's a problem, but it's too expensive. I don't know how to address it. It's going to cost me a lot of money. I'm getting along OK. I'm not really hurting as far as I know. Let's pass it until something..."

Of course, a very pervasive answer which strikes right at the heart of many people in this room is, "I recognize it's a problem, but *mental* health? That means I have to start dealing with shrinks and do-gooder social workers, and bleeding hearts, and people who have no understanding of what it is to earn a profit in today's world."

I come back to my question of whether I'm the star or the street cleaner. It's a matter of perspective.

Of course it is a problem. And a discerning manager and a discerning management will, of course, address it assiduously. We all know the oft-quoted statistic that in any given work force, 15 percent of employees in any given year will present themselves with emotional and behavioral problems. We all know the statistic that 8 to 10 percent of a work force is involved seriously and significantly with alcohol or substance abuse.

By the way, should we be talking about alcoholism in dealing with mental health? A Federal district court judge in Minnesota has ruled that alcoholism is not a mental health problem but rather "a physiologic disease." Of course, the underlying reason for that was the attempt of a group of alcoholism residential facilities to get Medicaid reimbursement when the Feds cut back their mental health support. Medicaid does not provide assistance for mental illness. So the facilities went to court and said the AMA says that alcoholism is a disease, the court adjudicated that it *is* a disease, and now it's eligible for Medicaid, at least in the Minnesota district. It is projected that if that decision were applicable around the country—and it's likely to be decided by the Supreme Court sooner or later—the Federal share of Medicaid will go up by $2.5 million a year. This gives you an idea of the magnitude of the alcohol problem, and that's just Medicaid's share of the cost.

It is a problem. Absenteeism, accidents, lost productivity, waste, and so on. And, of course, the environment is a very real problem and a very significant one, and one generating growing awareness. Let's not forget also that in our desire to control the environment, we don't go to the other extreme and create needless anxiety about the environment. We do have the Love Canal syndrome, and the Three Mile Island syndrome, and we do have mass psychogenic illness. These have been well-documented cases. Another example of a needless cause for anxiety was engendered by a report that those who work with visual display terminals run the risk of developing cataracts. Scientific evidence shows that there is no cataract danger, there's no radiation danger, and indeed, the problems relating to the VDT's have to do with the organization of work and the way the equipment is installed rather than the terminals themselves.

A key aspect of the problem is its enlargement beyond the employee who's complaining, or the individual with a family problem, to the disruption of the entire workforce. All of you, I'm sure, have had the experience of a co-worker troubled by a sick spouse, or a misbehaving child, or a serious family problem, bringing that problem into the plant and finding that work is disrupted because people are involved in the problem. There is endless discussion and gossip, and there are any number of telephone calls to get information about help and assistance for this individual. Of course, when it's a senior executive in the company who's worried about placing a spouse or a relative in a nursing home or in a psychiatric institution, then the whole company is involved in finding out what's going on and how to resolve this problem.

One of these problems is the need for child care. This is often very troublesome, and a number of organizations are paying attention to it.

In the New York Business Group on Health we are looking ahead 10 or 15 years in a project that relates to industry's responsibility for the employee who is a caregiver for a frail, elderly relative, or someone who's chronically disabled. If you look at the demographic changes that are going to take place in the next 10 or 20 years, you will recognize that it is going to be a very serious and pervasive problem. We're not saying it's the responsibility of industry to take care of the 80-year old individual. But that 80-year old individual is very often the parent of the 50-year old worker, and if we want to keep that worker healthy and functioning productively, we have to know what industry can do to provide the kind of support that's needed to sustain that individual in dealing with that problem. And it takes more than money.

Having acknowledged the problems, what are we going to do about them? Well, the medical model says we identify the person who's hurting, we diagnose the problem, we offer counseling, and we refer. It sounds simple and it is. But who identifies? Who bells the cat? It's easy for the supervisor to recognize and confront the fact that a worker who reports to him or her has a problem. But suppose it's the executive vice-president? Or even the chief executive officer who has the problem? Who bells the cat?

Supervisor training is an essential element in dealing with people problems that impact on work relationships. We need to sensitize our supervisors and our managers to them. The point I make is that training in addressing people problems should not be limited to supervisors but should be incorporated at all levels of management. Indeed, only now a few of the schools that turn out M.B.A.'s are offering at least some elective courses in human relations and how to handle these problems. These are long overdue.

Who does the counseling? In some large organizations there's a virtual holy war going on. Is counseling done by the occupational health department, the employees' health service? Is it done by personnel, human relations? There's an employees' counseling program—we now call them that; they're no longer called "employee assistance programs"— next month, there'll be another name for it. It's often set up as an independent entity. And sometimes, an employee with a problem is virtually torn to bits by fighting over who has the responsibility to look after it. I think that all these helpers do splendid work, and there are good reasons why one should be in one place in the organization and another in a different place in the organization. Because of the nature of the personnel or the labels on their doors, they attract different people with different kinds of problems. But they certainly should work together in a cooperative fashion.

Now, the issue of referrals. To whom do you refer? It's an awfully big world out there. Let me emphasize that much more important than *to* whom you refer the individual with a problem is *how* you refer. A very serious deficiency in many of the courses in counseling is that when they talk about referral, they don't teach how to refer. This is quite applicable to physicians and even psychologists and psychiatrists. They love to be on the receiving end, but they literally fall flat on their faces when it comes to being on the delivery end.

Another issue that needs to be looked at is the role of the employer when the person in trouble is a dependent of the employee. Can we bring these problems into the plant, or how do we extend the influence of the employer out into the family and into the community?

All right, we've got the individual referred and in treatment. But treatment costs money; who pays for it? None of you is sufficiently affluent, I believe, or so dedicated that you're ready to work for nothing, at least for not a substantial amount of time. This is a critical issue which The New York Business Group on Health has addressed through workshops on mental health benefits at which we discussed the question of whether there should be mental health benefits, and what their range should be, and so on. Member companies produced data showing that the use of psychiatric benefits is increasing at an alarming rate, even with a ceiling on the extent of the benefits. It's revealing, for example, that psychiatric hospitalization lasts as long as the period of coverage by the benefits: if it's 30 days, patients get cured in 30 days, and if it's 365 days, they stay in the hospital for a year. And, in many instances, there's really no indication that the results are any better no matter where they went, or for how long. In one company, the psychiatric hospital bills are now close to 20 percent of all of the hospital bills for all illnesses among their large population of covered employees and dependents. The average cost per admission for psychiatric illness was double that of the average cost of cardiac disease, including bypass surgery. It's 50 percent higher than the average cost for *all* disorders.

Health care benefit costs for large companies are escalating at the rate of 15 to 25 percent a year. Small businesses this year are getting increases in their health insurance premiums ranging from 50 to 150 percent.

One of the problems that we're dealing with is the question of extending benefits for people who are being separated. It has been suggested that the employer should continue health benefits for individuals for a long period while they're unemployed, a time when they can't afford to pay premiums out of their own pockets. Indeed, the United Auto Workers have negotiated a contract stipulating that if you have 20 years of service, your health benefits will continue almost indefinitely, paid for by management. But the problem is that if you have a company that's wavering on the brink and has to cut its payroll costs in order to stay alive, continuing health insurance benefits for all of the unemployed may dictate laying off additional employees in order to get the resources to pay that cost. It's an issue that I won't solve for you; it's a knotty one.

Again, on the subject of mental health, I've indicated that the treatment is often too long, and there are questionable modalities of therapy. Somebody recently made a study of the number of new modalities of group therapy that have been introduced in the last 10 years; I think they stopped somewhere at around 150. We see treatment without clear diagnostic indications, or even without a defined diagnosis. One of the serious problems in emotional and mental behavioral illness is what kind of label do you put on it? And of course, there is the other side of the issue, do we want to stigmatize people by putting labels on them? It's not easy to resolve.

Then there is the question of the use of psychiatric benefits not for illness but for things that are really self-improving, educational activities. How many in this audience have undertaken analysis or interpersonal therapy as part of a training program, and paid for it out of somebody's health benefits? Should that not have been a tuition charge?

Legislation is constantly being introduced in Albany and elsewhere to mandate certain psychiatric benefits and mandate the levels of coverage. At the same time, laws are being introduced to mandate the reimbursement of new kinds of providers in independent practice—social workers, psychologic counselors, nurses, faith healers—should they all be reimbursed? Should they all be encouraged to set up practice? An interesting phenomenon is the argument that all of these people are effective; they do just as well and they charge much less than psychiatrists. But once they have their diploma on the wall and are seeing patients, one hears the plea, "Why pay us less just because we have a different kind of diploma? We're doing the same work, we're helping the same patient, the patient gets better. Pay us on the basis of the diagnosis and the treatment." And somehow, that level seems always to gravitate to the top of the scale.

All this leaves those involved in managing health benefits in a very difficult position. How do you evaluate the validity of a claim for mental health benefits? The American Psychiatric Association presently has a peer review program in an attempt to adjudicate some of these problems relating to mental health benefits.

There is a new wrinkle. Presently, outpatient psychiatric benefits, as with most benefits, come into play only after you've spent enough money to meet the deductible. They tend to be limited in terms of the co-payments; that is, psychiatric benefits tend to be limited to 50 percent rather than 80 percent of the "reasonable" fee for other health services. And, generally, there's a ceiling of $5,000, $10,000, $20,000, depending on the plan, as a maximum either per year or per lifetime.

There is evidence that this discourages people from

getting into psychiatric care—the new approach is to "front-end" the benefit, to offer very limited, short-term treatment on a first-dollar coverage basis, with full coverage for the first four or five visits. There's already enough of a barrier in terms of stigma, concern, fear, anxiety, and difficulty in getting people into appropriate mental health therapy. This plan removes the financial barrier, at least long enough to get patients in treatment long enough to establish whether they really need it, to determine what kind of therapy they really need, and to be sure that they get referred appropriately.

A major argument being put forward in favor of that kind of liberality, if you call it liberality, is that a great deal of mental illness turns up in the ordinary benefit area. How many cases of alcoholism—and they account for over 50 percent of the hospitalizations in New York hospitals—are really labelled as alcoholic admissions? It's gastritis, it's stomach upset, it's brain syndrome, it's cirrhosis, and you-name-it. How many people are receiving treatment under medical benefits for what are really emotional and behavioral illnesses? The real danger is that they get into the hands of health professionals who treat them medically, subject them to batteries of costly tests, give them a lot of medication, diets, and treatment—all of which tend to make them sick—instead of paying attention to what the patient is saying. Our health professionals need to be taught to listen when people say, "I'm hurting," and to begin to ask why, and what could it be, rather than where does it hurt?

Well, so far, I've been guilty of exactly what the others have been doing, and that is talking about the medical model; identify, diagnose, and treat. Find the one who's hurting, and treat him. In terms of dealing with industry and management, especially in relation to mental health, we must focus primarily on prevention rather than treatment. We must not only identify the person who's sick, but we must identify potential problems and defuse them by appropriate preventive measures.

In doing this, we must face hard reality. There are choices and compromises that must be made. Do we expand health benefits or do we hire more workers? Or, the reverse side of that coin, do we cut back benefits, do we call for give-back on the part of the workers, or do we dismiss more workers? At a critical point, it's the survival of the enterprise which is at stake. And what kind of sacrifices must or should be made in order to keep that enterprise afloat?

Our goal is to keep the enterprise going, but, at the same time to reduce the human cost in terms of impaired well-being. The essence of that is respect for the inherent value of human dignity based on a respect for oneself as well as respect for others, a consistent, equitable value system, open communication and sharing of information, and a willingness to share problems, and rewards if we expect to share the pain.

When cutbacks are necessary—and they often are— let's at least make them clean. If we've got to amputate, at least let's use a reasonable anesthetic; let's use a sharp knife instead of a dull saw. Let's salvage as much human dignity as we can. Companies are realizing that and beginning to pay a lot of attention to "outplacement," now becoming a professional buzz word. There are now experts in outplacement who advise about retraining, help the individual find a new job, give him an opportunity to vent his justifiable anger at the employer who's throwing him out and casting him aside, and help him and his family survive this very traumatic experience. Most important of all, to help the employer avoid the ripple effects; the greatest damage from loss of jobs and the most difficult period is not to those who are let go, but to those who stay in continuing anxiety about the fear of losing their jobs.

Management needs help. Enlightened management—and the number of enlightened managements is growing continuously—needs reassurance. They are concerned about extensive long-term commitments. They're buying a product, a commodity, a service, which is quite new to management. If you want to sell services to them, don't put them to the test of expecting to get a lifetime commitment at this point, to buy the whole pizza pie. One slice at a time may be enough. Maybe that's all you can sell.

Where does management look for help? Well, some large organizations can afford to go out into the market and hire health professionals as consultants, or put them on salary. But many organizations have neither the resources nor the interest in doing that; they look to the community. And the community is South Oaks, and similar institutions, as well as many of the health professionals here.

How do they hire a health professional? How would you sell your services to industry? One thinks first of professional qualifications. What are the qualifications and who judges them? The question of formal accreditation becomes very important. But even more important than the curriculum vitae is the skill and personality of the individual. There needs to be some demonstration of that beyond a sales brochure. And the most significant element is a capacity for empathy. It's astonishing how many lack that as part of their professional makeup and their special capabilities.

I spoke earlier of doctrinaire attitudes and viewpoints. When I went to medical school that's what they trained me in, and those who went on into psychiatry got a post-graduate education in being authoritarian. Rightly, that puts many employers off.

Another question is availability. I have brochures on my desk from an organization that's setting itself up as a crisis resolution service, offering a full-range of mental health capabilities—psychiatrists, psychologists, social workers, counselors, and so on—ready to serve your needs. "Any time there's a crisis pick up the phone, call us, and we can give you immediate service"—at least during business hours. Well, I called them and got a recorded message: "We're sorry, we can't take your call now, but if you'll wait for the tone and leave your name and number, we'll have somebody call you back." Now, put yourself in the mind of an employee of an organization that's made a contract with this group to provide emergency services, who finally gets up enough nerve and enough desperation to call this number and say, "I'm calling for help." To get a machine? A machine that says give me your name and number and somebody will call you back?

A critical concern of the employer who is looking for these services is their price. I've had a number of people ask me, "How do I price my services?" The answer is, "Somewhere in the middle." If you charge too much, you'll frighten people off; if you charge too little, you'll be selling yourself too cheaply and you'll be dissatisfied. How do you know where the middle is? Feel your way: it sometimes depends on the competition, or on how hungry you are. You've got to get away from the idea that it's what the traffic will bear, because that will push you off the road immediately.

The most important element that you can bring is an understanding of the work world. Unfortunately, very few mental health professionals have an understanding of the business world. What is the meaning of work? How central is it in the individual's life? What does it mean to the individual, what does it mean to the family, what does it mean to the organization? Health professionals often lack understanding of the structure of an organization that's hiring them. What kind of a company is it? What kind of a business? How is it organized? What's its management style? What's its decision-making process? If you have no interest in these things, if all you've got is a billboard saying I'm the greatest genius in the field of mental health, my services are a godsend to humanity, all you have to do is hire me and I will solve all your problems, that's fine—if you believe it; not many others will.

I keep telling physicians and nurses, mental health professionals and others who want to work in industry, to sit in on some courses in a business school and learn about management principles, organization, and style. At least learn the buzz words and have a sense of what goes on.

But the most important element, the thing that in the last analysis most managements will look for is personal and professional integrity. The ability to be nonjudgmental, and the ability to be fair. To be fair to the organization, and be fair to the employee. To be fair to the family, and be fair to the community. In any job that I've had in industry, management has clearly understood that I'm impartial. And management has clearly understood that if it becomes a toss-up between the welfare of the employee and the welfare of the organization, the employee gets the benefit of my views and my advocacy. That's always been readily accepted.

In conclusion, let me emphasize that industry is becoming increasingly concerned with the health and well-being of its employees and their dependents. While its attention is aroused by the continuing escalation of health benefit costs, it quickly learns of the broad impact of health problems on morale, productivity, and profitability. Programs to alleviate distress and to control people problems are earning wider acceptance, and industry is becoming more sophisticated in evaluating and installing them. While the spread of these programs has been inhibited by economic factors, they are continuing to win acceptance. Much remains to be done, however, to improve their effectiveness, to tailor them to the needs of particular organizations and groups of employees, and to teach industry to use them most effectively. That is a challenge—and an opportunity—for all of us.

SELECTED READING

Addison-Wesley Series on Occupational Stress

House, J.S., *Work Stress and Social Support*
Levi, L., *Preventing Work Stress*
McLean, A.A., *Work Stress*
Moss, L., *Management Stress*
Shostak, A.B., *Blue Collar Stress*
Warshaw, L.J., *Managing Stress*

Akabus, S.H. and Kurzman, P.A. eds., *Work, Workers and Work Organizations*, Englewood Cliffs, NJ, Prentice Hall, 1982

Dorian, R. ed., *Adapting to a Changing World*, Ottawa, Quality of Working Life Unit, Canadian Ministry of Labour, 1981

Kanter, R.M., *Work and Family in the United States*, New York, Russell Sage Foundation, 1977

DISCUSSION

Chaired by speaker Dr. Warshaw, this panel included: Irving L. Hammerschlag, M.D., Medical Director, Long Island Lighting Company: Patricia K. Herman, R.N., M.S., Assistant Administrator, Psychiatric Services, University

Hospital at Stony Brook; Donald W. Sneller, Minister, Community Methodist Church; and Edward R. Sodaro, Jr., M.D., Staff Psychiatrist, South Oaks Hospital.

Ms. Herman:

I have always been interested in the needs of the worker, and now as a hospital administrator, I have the responsibility for examining stress in the workplace. At the same time, I have a responsibility to see that the workplace runs efficiently. Often, as clinicians, we're caught in the middle in terms of providing help to the worker, and at the same time being responsible to administration. I think there's often a conflict there.

Dr. Hammerschlag:

As the medical director of LILCO, my job is to look after the health and well-being of 6,000 employees.

Rev. Sneller:

I approach this subject from two viewpoints. Years ago I owned an industrial electrical construction company and two retail stores, so I worked as management. Presently, I'm the pastor of a 700-member church, and the families in this church represent a cross-section of the community.

Dr. Sodaro:

My concerns are in problems of psychiatric private health insurance, and in the context of this meeting, what efforts, if any, health promotion can have in reducing the costs of psychiatric benefits.

Audience:

Would anyone care to comment on quality circles as a way to involve the work group, increase productivity, and promote better mental health.

Dr. Warshaw:

I can respond to that, having been involved. Quality circles is a buzzword for a form of worker involvement which had its origins primarily in Scandinavia where it was known as "worker democracy." The idea is very simple. It was picked up by the Japanese very early on, and has come back in full bloom. It's quite popular in Canada and increasingly popular in this country.

The essence of quality circles is to reduce the alienation and separation of the worker from management and from control of the job. The quality circle is really a technique of group dynamics—bringing together the workers in a unit and their supervisor, and occasionally top management people, for freewheeling discussions of the work, the way they do it, and the way it's organized. This gives workers an opportunity to critique the work flow, work structure, the workplace, the work machinery, and also the division of labor. The classic experiment, I think, is the famous one at the Volvo auto plant. It involved a modification of the assembly line.

You've all seen at least pictures of an assembly line and you recognize that this is one of the most stressful occupations in the sense of people doing mechanical tasks, doing them to the pacing of a machine which they cannot control, and usually at a noise level that precludes any communication from one worker to another. On an assembly line, even the most basic human necessities must give way to that assembly line—if you have to go to the bathroom, you have to hold up your hand and wait for the foreman or supervisor to recognize you and get somebody to hold your spot while you go off so that the work will not be interrupted. Truly dehumanizing.

At the Volvo plant, the quality circles resulted in breaking the assembly line workers into teams. They put the cars in bays and had a multiplicity of teams brought together. The teams themselves had meetings and they decided who was going to do which piece of the operation. They discovered, after a period of time, that they were producing more cars with fewer defects and enjoyed a much higher level of worker satisfaction. These teams continued to meet, so that it was entirely possible for them to rotate jobs, either several times during the course of the day or, if one fellow liked a particular task he could stick with it. If he liked being a welder and only wanted to weld, fine, as long as that was acceptable to his co-workers; he did only the welding, whereas the others could change jobs often.

That kind of movement has been spreading very rapidly. "Experts" on quality circles will sell you their consulting services on how to organize quality circles in your plant. It does involve some expertise in terms of managing group dynamics. Some unions and workers are concerned that quality circles is another mechanism for exploiting workers and getting more work out of them per unit of time. But the essence of the quality circles is that it gives the individual a "piece of the action," an opportunity to have a say about what he or she does on the job, how they do it, and how it relates to their co-workers. It's threatening to management in some organizations; it's threatening to some unions who see it as relinquishing their prerogatives. Very often, before it can be introduced into a unionized plant, unions, labor, and management must meet to set ground rules and make sure that the quality circle is not the place to air labor grievances.

But it is a dynamic movement and a successful one. It works very well both in large and small organizations if it's done right. It is not a panacea, but it is a very useful instrument if it's understood and accepted and there's a commitment to it. There are very often some very definite short-term gains, and this can lead to complacency—if so, it tends to fall apart rather quickly. It has to be built in and continued. Generally when it's brought into an organization and it starts in one unit or one operation, it generally spreads through word of mouth because of the satisfaction of those involved in it. When it works well, the other workers want to get a piece of that action.

Audience:

I'd like to hear your comments on the value of outplacement counseling for those workers who are about to lose their jobs or who *have* lost their jobs.

Ms. Herman:

I've seen several situations where companies have been taken over and there was a great management shake-up. These companies brought in consultants to help these outplaced individuals find other jobs. I think that was most helpful, because the consultants dealt with a lot of the ripple effect from losing one's job—getting re-trained for other jobs, going through the hassle of redoing resumes, role-playing, applying for other jobs. There's a terrible feeling in an institution when there is a shake-up. Even those who are not in danger of losing their jobs feel the potential for job loss. I think it is important for the manager, then, to deal with these feelings and bring the situation out into the open where everyone can talk about it.

Dr. Sodaro:

I think the type of counseling depends on the reason for the employee's potential dismissal. If the employee is suffering from a bonafide psychiatric illness—and not just a question of incompetence—then I think that it definitely merits an attempt at salvaging the employee. Many people don't recognize just how salvageable a person is through proper care. This can be particularly documented by research on alcoholism and other psychiatric conditions. The answer to your question depends in part on the nature of the person's problem. If it is a psychiatric condition, they should be referred prior to dismissal.

Dr. Warshaw:

Yes, I think that's very important. I think that the traditional out-placement service is useful to a limited degree in that it offers help in formulating a resume, getting business cards printed, and providing some very superficial guidance. That has some validity. Beyond that, however, true *career* counseling is very important. For many, a change of job represents an opportunity for a new career, and so the more successful out-placement firms offer intensive career counseling—an analysis of one's capabilities, one's likes and dislikes, and the opportunity to strike out in a completely different direction, other than just another job.

They provide a realistic assessment of the labor market and a direction in terms of where to go. We have too many examples of splendid workers going down to the Sun Belt to get those new high-paying high-tech jobs. And we know how many are slipping back, having exhausted their resources because those jobs just aren't there. So it's a question of realistic counseling and realistic appraisal of the market.

There's another inherent element from the mental health standpoint; this is why it's so important to have out-placement counselors with some mental health training, or at least some counseling skills. The most important element in out-placement counseling is restoration of the self-esteem and sense of self-worth that the individual has had damaged. No matter how long you've been on the job and no matter how you've hated it, if the decision to leave is not yours, it generates a sense of rejection, and this is a blow to the self-esteem. The opportunity to rebuild one's ego and sense of self-worth and to do it realistically is extremely valuable.

When I was at the Equitable, we had closed down a particular unit; the sad part was that that unit had to be closed down at a time when other parts of the company were expanding. A psychologist in our medical department set up group sessions for those being out-placed. The value of providing a group mental health therapy environment was that these individuals could vent much of their hostility and bring in to the sessions the concerns of their spouses and children in relation to what was happening.

This raises one very important question: should the out-placement program be *part* of the organization, or should it be *outside* the organization? The rationale for having it inside the organization is that the counselors very often know the out-placed workers and understand, like, and respect them. On the other hand, counselors are part of the management of the organization that's laying off these employees so some of the resentment may rub off on them. In many instances, it's better to have the counselors come from a totally neutral source.

Audience:

I'd like to ask a question about a population we haven't talked about much—the emerging work force. How do we deal with those people who are just coming out of college with their B.A.'s, or just coming out of trade schools, and are trying to find work at the same time that their fathers, perhaps, are being laid off.

Ms. Herman:

Well, in a hospital situation, I think it's most important that there are orientation and training programs and an active involvement of getting new workers placed in the right part of the organization.

Dr. Warshaw:

The great problem lies in the inferior education that they've had and the fact that they have few skills to offer. Their skills are rudimentary. At the Equitable, we maintained a half a floor which was nothing but classrooms where we taught basic arithmetic, spelling, English, typing, and what not, to graduates of some of our better high schools and business schools. Even college graduates sometimes were enrolled in those courses because they needed the training.

A particularly important element of the new generation of workers is a kind of lackadaisical attitude toward what we consider "work readiness." "Work readiness" is an understanding of what it means to work; that work is essentially a contract between an employee and an employer. The employer says, "I'm going to give you a job and you will do certain things and we will compensate you in a certain way." And the employee says, "I will do my best to be there to do the job as well as I can within reason, and to perform the useful work which you assigned me to do within the limits of my ability."

The basic problem with many young people is that they know *nothing* about getting to work on time; playing hookey as they used to do in school is translated into a terrible attendance record on the job. That "work readiness" and work understanding has been especially important in terms of the rehabilitation of drug abusers and alcoholics, particularly young people, who go through institutional treatment in community agencies where getting them a job is the end role. One of the problems we have with many of these agencies is that they put these people back into the labor market without having inculcated in them the concept of regularity of work habits, which is essential, no matter the job.

Dr. Hammerschlag:

The other side of the coin is an individual who has put in 25 years with a corporation and finds that he is physically unable to continue doing what he's been doing. This is both an economic disaster and an emotional disaster for him. I frequently see individuals who have been in physical jobs that would pose a danger if they were to continue because of health problems. We suggest—and sometimes insist—that they change jobs. In the majority of cases they don't want to change because change represents a loss in self-confidence. People who come back to work after coronaries, for example, who have done physical work, come back, and our company is very magnanimous; we do not change their economic status but we do change their physical status. Emotionally, this is tremendously traumatic to some.

Ms. Herman:

I think the key in working with young, inexperienced workers as well as older workers, is a well-trained supervisor who understands "people problems" as well as the needs of the organization. In my experience, there isn't enough preparation for supervisors today, especially in hospital situations.

Dr. Warshaw:

Well, the question of an "understanding and sympathetic supervisor" sometimes boomerangs. Very often the employee—and this deals with a person who has an emotional illness as well as those with physical incapacities—is protected and guarded by a kind, beneficent supervisor who overlooks the deficiencies of the individual as long as the rest of the unit makes up for it. That is, the supervisor overlooks them until something happens to a second person or a third person in the unit and the supervisor's neck is on the line because the work isn't getting done. Very often, that beneficent kindness is converted into a resentment: "I've covered up for this fellow and now he's letting me down." Very often, that kindness is converted into virtual brutality in trying to unload this anchor, this millstone. That's why I emphasize that supervisory training in human problems is not only learning to be sensitive to the fellow who drinks too much, or who has been beating his wife, but rather in terms of human behavior in *all* aspects of the work situation.

Audience:

I see a basic conflict here in the problem of the corporation. It's basically a problem of management versus therapy. For example, is it legitimate for corporations to have ongoing training programs to try to deal with personality problems? Or, is it more important for corporations to have a "hard-nosed management" that deals with organizational problems?

Rev. Sneller:

I don't think it's an either/or situation. We talk about treating the *whole* person; the whole person has to do with the problems that the employee has with his or her spouse, or with the children. Should management be responsive to that baggage which the employee brings on the job? Perhaps, but there are some networks that the employee may have, too—the temple or synagogue or church—and very often management is not aware of the resources of the religious community. In this area alone, there are a half-dozen parishes that have clinically trained clergy and counselors.

I've known many persons over the last five years who have gone through job loss. I put them in touch with each other as a support system that helps them realize it's OK to be angry as hell. It's OK to be anxious but you are going to move through that process.

There are resources beyond management.

Dr. Warshaw:

Dr. Hammerschlag, how do you handle it?

Dr. Hammerschlag:

I don't think you can make any generalizations as to what the appropriate response for a corporation should be. If I'm in business for myself and I have two employees and one of them develops an emotional problem which is going on *ad infinitum*, I can't live with him. But if I'm an employer with 17,000 employees and five of them get sick, I can afford to go along with their particular problem for as long as possible.

There are limitations on both sides. Our company makes every serious effort to be helpful. We have a counselor, we have an alcoholic program, we have an open-door policy in the medical department. But there are limitations, and occasionally the situation requires that you decide how long you're going to carry that employee.

Dr. Warshaw:

There is, indeed, built into the situation a kind of schizoid problem. On one hand the company desires to be helpful, and on the other hand there is the necessity of staying in business and maintaining revenue flow. That's something that each organization has to decide for itself. But the important thing is that in larger organizations it can work. But it has to work by first establishing a written policy which states this is what we will do and this is how far we will go. This must be developed not at a time of crisis when some acute situation has everybody concerned, but well in advance. The policy can't be chiseled in granite because it must be modified over time. But the policy must be stated and the commitment clearly understood. By the way, it's an awfully good idea to have labor representatives and employee representatives participate in the drafting of that policy.

Secondly, having established a policy it must be advertised throughout the organization in language that people understand. In some organizations in this area, it will require tri-lingual duplication. This policy must be implemented equitably, fairly, and firmly throughout the company. If that is done, the company is comfortable and the employees are comfortable.

Most importantly, the company *behavior* must be consistent with the policy. If the company says, we are going to be concerned about mental illness but doesn't provide benefits to pay for mental care, that's inconsistency. If the company takes a firm rule with respect to alcoholism but has a bar in its executive dining room, that doesn't make sense. If a company offers lectures on health promotion and good nutrition and then serves nothing but junk food in its vending machines, there's an inconsistency.

There are three things necessary for good policy: It must be well-developed, well-understood, by all involved; the policy must be advertised so that everybody understands it; and it must be consistent and equitable in its application.

Audience:
We talked about the frustration of the young people coming out of school and not being able to find employ-

ment. I'm a nursing home administrator and I have a lot of people asking me for jobs. When I ask them what experience they have, they invariably have none. I think the schools have failed miserably in educating youngsters as to how they should approach getting a job. I think one of the most wonderful ways youngsters can get job experience is by doing volunteer work. Over the years, our nursing home has had volunteers who found that they liked nursing homes, and directed their education in that direction. When they leave us, they have actual experience which they can use in finding employment.

Audience:

I am a provider of EAP services at a psychiatric hospital and I'd like to know what is going to happen with the kinds of services I provide if management decides to go to flexible benefits.

Dr. Warshaw:

Flexible benefits are a method for introducing competition into the health scheme whereby an employee is offered a choice of multiple benefits schemes, some more comprehensive than others, but involving a greater cost in terms of a worker's payroll deduction which goes for his share of the benefits. There's such a thing as "cafeteria benefits" in which he's given a whole tray-full of benefit programs in which he can assemble his own personal benefit package based upon his needs and his pocketbook.

In terms of employee counseling programs, or EAP's, there are several arrangements that are made. In a number of instances, the employer will contract with the EAP service to provide, at employer's expense, a certain number of initial visits for counseling, evaluation, and then referral, with the employee then picking up the rest of the tab with the help of the benefits coverage, if any. In some cases, the employee is expected to pay for it entirely out of pocket, again with the help of any benefits that may exist.

The future isn't clear. Companies increasingly are looking at their benefit packages, and I must tell you that there is a tendency among insurance consultants and those who have been burned by rather extensive over-utilization of psychiatric benefits, to cut way back on mental health coverage. Of course, it's very easy to save benefits costs by removing benefits. But in doing so, you lose track of the essential purpose of the benefits scheme which is to provide protection against costs that the individual cannot readily meet on his own. And so one constantly upsets balance.

I do find a growing interest in employee counseling programs. There's a growing tendency to have them provided by outside groups rather than installing them within companies simply because it avoids the long-term commitment to personnel. It's a lot easier to get your feet wet without making a capital commitment, or salary commitment over a long period of time. It seems quite clear that employee counseling programs are becoming more and more popular and their value is becoming increasingly appreciated.

On the other hand, the field is getting more and more crowded, in the sense that more and more psychiatric hospitals and general hospitals and psychiatrists, psychologists, and social workers are forming their own counseling services. There are now entrepreneurial concerns that market counseling services and then hire health professionals to deliver the services. Thus we have a rising demand, but at the same time we have a growing number of people who are not only eager to meet that demand but are going out proselytizing to increase it. Where it's going to wind up, I don't know.

Dr. Sodaro:

Sometimes the term "consumer's choice" is also used for flexible benefits. It is often proposed that a particular array of policies be offered, and employees choose among these policies. The employees choosing the cheaper policies might receive a cash bonus at the end of the fiscal year. The problem with this, of course, is that individuals would be rewarded financially for choosing inadequate health care for themselves and their families. This doesn't just apply to psychiatric benefits, it includes such things as dental care and preventive medicine.

If you're going to cut back on treatments for periodontal disease, cardiovascular stress testing, or alcohol counseling, you're going to pay a high financial price at a future date. It's an example of seeking short-term savings while ignoring long-term implications of benefits to both management and employees.

As far as psychiatric benefits are concerned the cheaper proposed policies are modeled after Medicare which severely discriminates against psychiatric patients. In my opinion consumer choice or flexible benefits are misnomers.

If one is stuck with an inadequate policy in regard to psychiatric benefits, you're simply dumping the problems when they develop to another treatment source. Instead of private facilities being available, one is referred to a state hospital and the employee there will require hospitalization, which is quite expensive to business, ultimately, in taxes.

Audience:

We addressed ourselves to the entrance in the labor market and the exit in the labor market. I would like to address this to the person in the middle, the person who has worked for many years in either industry or in an agency, and who has educated himself, and who is neglected. I'm referring to a person who is spending much time obtaining a master's degree or a doctorate, and is not being recognized by his agency or by industry. He is fuming inside, not getting anywhere. I think the agency or industry should recognize that these people exist among them and the company must address themselves to alleviating the neglect.

Dr. Hammerschlag:

You're absolutely right. I can see a very close parallel to young people who are over-qualified. Here is an individual who obtains a job and really outgrows it over a period of years. They go for their master's, and perhaps even a doctorate. That relates to a young person who finishes school and thinks his B.S. degree isn't enough so he goes on for a master's, goes on for a Ph.D. and finds out there are no jobs for him.

Ms. Herman:

I've seen many situations where an individual who has gone to school, who has upgraded himself and not received any recognition is being treated as the troublemaker in the institution. And when you're treated as a troublemaker, generally you are. I think the best way to handle it is for the manager to take some sense of responsibility and let that person know just why they're not moving up in the organization, and help them look for something that's more viable for them.

Dr. Warshaw:

When there is a good performance evaluation program in which an employee can sit down periodically with a trained supervisor to appraise not only performance but the job, that's a good time to talk about future possibilities within the organization. In many organizations, promotions are made available on an open-posting basis; all new openings, all job placements have to be posted so that everybody in the organization has an opportunity to bid for it. There are a number of ways in which this problem can be resolved. In many instances, however, it calls for explicitly sensitive counseling on the part of the individual, because there may be a disparity between one's self-worth—in the sense of my own evaluation of what I'm doing and the quality of my work in the job—and a somewhat different evaluation of the worth of that work and that output on the part of the organization.

I beg the question as to who is right. But clearly the individual who finds himself in that situation ought to find some counseling that will provide at least an opportunity for a more objective appraisal and an opportunity for ventilation. That will lead, I think, to appropriate decision-making.

Audience:

I'm the director of a local parish center guidance and employment assistance program. Because of de-institutionalization of patients, we're getting a larger and larger group of people who have been released from institutions and we're having difficulty in finding assistance to place people in jobs. First of all, corporations take a risk in accepting this type of person, and we find that the institutions which released these people are sending them out without at least some idea of what they might have to face. We've had psychiatrists suggesting to their patients that now they are ready for some sort of part-time work, and they send them to us. It's very, very difficult to place a person of that nature. The contacts that we've developed with employers are at risk if we recommend an unskilled person.

I wonder if there's some way in which institutions can better prepare for the person's release on a level besides the psychiatric level, to prepare them or at least advise them of the problems that they face on the outside.

Are your corporations in some way able to take a risk with some of these patients?

Dr. Sodaro:

I think that's the $64,000 question: what to do with the de-institutionalized chronic patient.

Possibly one area that might be looked at is more aggressive and stronger financial incentives on the part of government to business to employ these de-institutionalized patients who do represent the possibility of significant financial drain on the company otherwise. It is not an easy area to deal with.

Dr. Warshaw:

Yes, there is risk-taking but quite a number of organizations in the private sector are willing to take on problem cases. There are organizations that will hire recovered alcoholics, "recovered" drug abusers, and even people coming out of the criminal justice system. Many companies do hire such people but they don't advertise it because they don't want to be inundated. There's a limit to what they can do.

One of the serious problems we have is that in the New York City area, there are an estimated one million people who need job training, who fit exactly the characteristics required for the Federally-supported CETA job-training program. With the present level of cutbacks for this fiscal year, the current CETA program can accommodate only 1,000. The state does not have a CETA program. The city as an employer of last resort has hired many people but the city has a budget to balance, and there's a limit to tax resources.

The answer lies not in special resources nor in advocacy for special programs. The problem is part of the total social fabric. What can we afford for our social programs? This is a national policy decision. The Reagan administration has taken a fairly firm position with respect to this. It remains for us as voters and citizens to react to that policy one way or the other.

Audience:

Do you feel that the only answer, then, is government-supported programs?

Dr. Warshaw:

No, I think it's a partnership problem. I don't think government can do it alone and I certainly don't think that private sector can fully make up for the deficiencies of government.

Audience:

I've been hearing the implication that providing counseling or other mental health services is a philanthropic matter. What hard-nosed benefits may businesses derive from employee counseling programs?

Ms. Herman:

Well, for one thing, I think *not* recognizing stress in the worker is going to cause the company problems, not only in high turnover and low productivity and morale problems, but possibly loss of the individual himself. I think it's most important that managers recognize what are the stresses for the worker in the organization and make attempts to change the stresses or allow employees to participate in looking at what is needed to alleviate the stress. In terms of providing therapy or counseling for the individual, I don't think that's the manager's responsibility at all. But the manager has to know who to refer to, and referral sources have to be available to him.

And managers have to be trained to know what kind of employee problems or people problems they're going to run into, and who the referral sources are.

Dr. Warshaw:

I think that any enterprise, be it for profit, government or not-for-profit, has to be run with some degree of efficiency. Even the helping organizations, regardless of how beneficent and magnanimous they may be to their clients, have to require a certain level of efficiency from their own staff and management if they're going to stay in business long. I believe I take a very hard-nosed attitude with respect to employee counseling programs. I say that charity is something which ought to be labelled as charity and put into the collection plate. There's no room for charity in operating and managing an organization. Very simply, employee counseling programs exist in the work place because it is good business. If you take any machine and run it without proper lubrication, it won't last long. The counseling program can serve as a lubricant to keep the parts working together smoothly. If it functions well, it can serve as an alarm system to identify problems within the organization or, indeed, units within the organization which are sources of potential explosions. Let me remind you also that a counseling program has a dual effect: it's therapeutic to the individual, to the client being treated and it's preventive for those individuals with whom that individual must work.

Audience:

It seems to me that a prime criterion for what defines mental health or mental illness in industry is cost-benefit to the company. My question, then, is what are the prime criteria that major industries use in defining what is mental health and what is mental illness?

Ms. Herman:

We have a variety of programs for employees, which hopefully helps their mental health, including preventive programs such as how to quit smoking and how to lose weight. On the lighter side we have a variety of exercise programs, aerobics and dancing. Our employee assistance program or counseling program is very active. The employees themselves are very involved in identifying what it is that they need and what kind of needs are not being met. Generally that's done every six months, when a questionnaire is sent to all employees asking what kinds of problems they're having in the organization and what kinds of things do they think would be helpful. Then, a committee composed of employees as well as managers, is set up to look at how we can provide some of these things that our employees look for.

Dr. Warshaw:

We've fallen into the trap of trying to justify thinking in terms of industry as bottom-line oriented; and indeed industries are. If the truth be known—and I'm as guilty as others of using all kinds of figures to demonstrate cost effectiveness—there are very few hard data on which I would place any reliability. Certainly there are very few control studies in terms of a cost benefit analysis. Much of what appears in the literature is indeed suspect. Here's a simple example: As an occupational physician, I sell my services to industry as a great expert in preventive medicine by offering flu shots. I guarantee them that I won't take any money unless I give them a 95 percent freedom from flu. There's just one small proviso: I want to give the shots in June, and I'll evaluate the results in August. If I had to give the shots in November, and then run the risk of winter viral episodes, I'd lose my shirt.

Very simply, management today has some sophistication and some understanding. They would not be where they are if they were simple figure people and simple accountants. They can grasp philosophy and they can understand abstractions. They can see the merit of these programs and the logic and the rationale for them without the hard numbers, without the hard data. This is not to say that they won't evaluate it. You have to be very convincing.

Audience:

I think it's probably safe to say that we have a way to go in regard to mental health programs in industry. There is a very useful array of negative responses on the part of many industrial leaders on why they can't or won't get engaged in mental health programs. Dr. Warshaw, does the New York Business Group on Health have a policy and program to respond to those negative responses?

Dr. Warshaw:

Yes. One of the cardinal thrusts of the New York Business Group on Health is employer education. Our members are all organizations and employers. Some are profit, some not-for-profit, some large, some small. One of the primary thrusts is to educate the employer in terms of more effective handling of health-related problems, health-related costs. This includes attention to benefits design and benefits administration and all the things relating to health insurance coverage. It includes counseling and providing opportunities for exchange of experiences with respect to employee health programs. We've published a manual on how to set up employee counseling programs.

We've run a special seminar on employee counseling programs for small businesses. We have a monthly newsletter in every issue of which you'll find no less than 10 or 12 hints, references, or articles on various forms of health promotion, various aspects of minimizing the costs of health benefits and the drain on the health system. We focus on prevention through articles encouraging employers to teach their employees and, through them, their dependents, better health maintenance and more inteligent utilization of the health care system, which includes the mental health system.

This is being accepted by companies. On the one hand, it stems from a degree of curiosity as to whether they shouldn't be doing this. On the other hand it comes from a conviction that they ought to be doing it, and they'd like to be doing it better.

Audience:

I would like to ask two questions together. One, what do you think of stress management and the plethora of stress management consultants? Two, would you discuss the need-to-know between management and the counseling therapists. How much information needs to go between them?

Dr. Warshaw:

The second question is very easy. What goes on between the employee and the counselor, whether that counselor is an employee of the company or an outside contractor, should be as confidential as any communication in the health field. *None* of it is to be revealed without the express knowledge and consent of the individual involved. In a number of companies that I've served as a consultant, there is an arrangement whereby individuals may go to a particular psychiatrist or to a counseling service outside

the company on their own volition, their own referral
without fear of being identified. The psychiatrist or counseling service knows that the company will pick up the tab
for a given number of visits on bills that are submitted
anonymously. This obviates the problems that I, as an employee, can go to you as a counseling service, and be sure
that what I tell you will be confidential. But in order for
you to get paid, you have to give the company my name
and a diagnosis and that blows the whole thing.

Another way of dealing with this problem lies in the
procedure of filing insurance claims for psychiatric care.
The usual track for benefit claims is that the employee fills
out the form, gives it to the therapist, who sends it to the
employer who verifies that the employee is still employed,
is covered under the company's program, and the particular program makes him eligible for those benefits. Then
it goes to an insurance company which pays the bill. Some
carriers provide the employer with a list of names of people
who filed claims. In some instances there is sufficient concern over being stigmatized for getting psychiatric therapy
that employees won't put in the claim.

One way to obviate that is to modify the procedure so
that the claim form goes to the personnel department *first*
to validate eligibility for the benefit. It *then* goes to the
health professional who fills out the claim form, who sends
it directly to the insurance company for processing that
claim by people who are far removed and totaly imper-
sonal. Carrier reports to the company provide only aggre-
gate information in which individuals cannot be identified.

Dr. Sodaro:
Studies have shown that 15 percent of all adults who
have psychiatric insurance choose not to utilize those benefits in favor of the strict privacy of a self-pay arrangement.
It seems clear, therefore, that there exists a large group

of employees who cannot afford out-of-pocket expenses but choose to neglect psychiatric disturbance in themselves or their families out of fear that their employer might somehow misuse the knowledge that they were utilizing these benefits.

Dr. Hammerschlag:

We have a system that works pretty well. We recently had a recovered alcoholic who became a counselor. He's a blue-collar worker who has made considerably more contact with the workers than the medical department has been able to. There has always been a certain amount of restraint. Employees are afraid that management is going to find out, despite the fact that it's always been in confidence. Now if you have a problem—alcohol or otherwise—you see our counselor. He will advise you where to go. If you go to the counselor with a medical problem, he would send you to the medical director. If you go to him with a psychiatric problem, he'll suggest you see our consulting psychiatrist. If you go to him with alcohol problems, the counselor handles it and does a rather good job. Nobody other than the individual who you seek out will know about it. If you require hospitalization, the counselor will ask permission to notify me, because I can get you OK'd to be absent from your department. A lot of it is a little ridiculous because if you work with six guys and you disappear for 31 days, they know where you are, but, it's worked out very well. We can do it because we're a large corporation.

Dr. Warshaw:

Confidentiality is a state of mind. Very often, those things the employee wishes to be kept confidential by the counselor or the physician are talked about in the cafeteria, in the elevator, in the parking lot. In many instances, if the truth were known it would be much less damaging than the rumor that's going around.

One of the problems that I had as a medical director was protecting the individual's job and holding it for him. We need to have some idea of prognosis with respect to how long that person is going to be out, and the likelihood of his being able to return to that job with safety to himself, his co-employees, and the public.

I think that we have to look at the issue of confidentiality from a variety of perspectives, and avoid rigid doctrinaire viewpoints. We must understand that if we have a formal policy that is clearly understood by everyone, then it's important for everyone to get together and work together without that policy on behalf of the individual.

Audience:

My understanding is that there are certain legitimate DSM-III diagnoses that are not reimbursable by insurance companies. I'm not quite certain how an EAP counselor would refer somebody for marital counseling.

Dr. Warshaw:

That depends on the particular insurance program. It depends on the state in which you're functioining. In some states, psychologists can be reimbursed and *have to be* reimbursed by law; in some states they do not. In some companies, insurance programs will reimburse psychiatrists and social workers in independent practice, others will not. There's an extreme variability.

Audience:

How does that affect an EAP provider?

Dr. Warshaw:

In some instances, the EAP service is paid for by the company, just like they buy a cleaning service, catering services, and so on. This is another service that they buy, and it has nothing to do with reimbursement.

Audience:

I thought that EAP would also be operating in a company that did have health insurance benefits.

Dr. Warshaw:

The point is that under some company insurance programs, treatment by an employee counseling service, *per se,* is not reimbursable. It is not covered by health insurance benefits because they will cover only treatments given by a formally accredited psychiatrist, and in some instances a formally accredited psychologist. Under such circumstances, the individual has to pay for it out-of-pocket, without the help of benefits. There is extreme variability and one has to look at the program in each company. I don't think you can base your program upon the assumption that your services will always be covered by insurance benefits.

Dr. Sodaro:

I think that psychiatrists have underplayed the seriousness of diagnosis as far as insurance forms are concerned. Studies by the National Institute of Mental Health have shown that in Washington, D.C., when psychiatrists were given an opportunity to anonymously provide diagnoses, 60 percent to 80 percent of the diagnoses were of major psychiatric illness, such as bipolar illness, or major depressive illness. On insurance forms, though, only 20 percent carried such diagnoses. So the issue of confidentiality is again raised. Apparently, psychiatrists are quite concerned about this.

Audience:

There is still a tremendous stigma attached to being either mentally ill or having an emotional problem and I think it is up to the mental health profession to eradicate this. What difference does it make if you have a problem in your head or in your foot? You're still sick. Why should you be ashamed that you employer is going to find out? This is what the issue of confidentiality boils down to. Why should anyone worry about someone finding out he or she is sick?

Dr. Hammerschlag:

I think the stigma is made by the individual who has the problem, not by medicine, and not by the general public. I think we're all aware that people have problems and I think these problems are magnified a thousand-fold by the individual who has this particular problem. An example is that people with problems in our corporation don't want to come to see me. They just don't want to come. Finally, I put together a program where we have a blue-collar counselor; in the last year he has seen 100 more people than I have been able to see. So the stigma is not on the part of the individual's fellow workers. The stigma is on the part of the individuals themselves.

Dr. Sodaro:

I believe that there is severe discrimination in insurance coverage for psychiatric patients and their problems. If you look at policies for individual companies, I think you'd find significant discrimination against psychiatric patients.

Dr. Warshaw:

There is really no stigma until somebody decides that there is. Keep in mind what has happened in an election campaign when it became known that one of the candidates had sometime in the past sought counseling for what was labelled as an emotional or mental problem. Suppose that you wanted to join the CIA, the FBI, or the State Department and they ask if you've ever been hospitalized or treated for an emotional or mental illness. There are situations in which it is very legitimate to be concerned about such a disclosure. If I'm riding in a supersonic jet along with 200 other passengers, it would be helpful to know that the pilot who's guiding my destiny for those few hours has been carefully screened, both in terms of his physical capability and his emotional ability to handle any crisis that might arise. There are special situations.

As Dr. Hammerschlag indicates, however, in most instances, it is a perception rather than a fact. It takes a long time to eradicate stigma from the minds of some people. That's why it's necessary in most organizations to go through the charade of an over-developed program to maintain confidentiality. We have to go through that charade so that people will believe that their confidentiality will not be betrayed.

INDEX